WHEN THE STONES CRY OUT

THE IMPORTANCE OF WORSHIPPING GOD, AND *END TIME PROPHECIES* TO HELP YOU PREPARE FOR THE RAPTURE AND RETURN OF JESUS CHRIST.

ELLEN JOUBERT

© Copyright 2019 Ellen Joubert
Published by Leading Voice International Pty Ltd

All rights reserved. No part of this book may be reproduced in any written, electronic, recording, or photocopying without the publisher or author's written permission. The exception would be in the case of brief quotations embodied in the critical articles or reviews and pages where the publisher or author grants explicit license. Every precaution has been taken to verify the accuracy of the information contained herein. The author and publisher assume no responsibility for any errors or omissions. No liability is accepted for damages that may result from the use of the information contained within.

Cover design by Mercedes Piñera.

ISBN:

Paperback
978-0-6485691-6-9

Ebook
978-0-6485691-9-0 (EPUB)

*I dedicate this book to all God's people.
May the reader be blessed and encouraged to
praise and worship Almighty God every day to receive
the fullness of His blessings.
May it inspire you to be ready for the Rapture .
and the Return of Jesus Christ our Lord and Saviour,
to be with Him in all eternity.*

Table of Contents

Acknowledgements 7
Foreword 9

Chapter 1. Why God Loves Us So Much 15
   Following Christ Develops our Character 17
   The Meaning of Being Born Again 21
   The Blood Sacrifice 24
   Prayer of Repentance 26

Chapter 2. Is God Real And Is The Bible Reliable? 27
   The Bible 28
   Five Reasons that Affirm the Bible 33

Chapter 3. The Enemies of Man &
                The Enemies of God 35
   The Enemies of Man 35
   The Enemies of God 35
   God is Light 40

Chapter 4. Spiritual Warfare 47
   The Battle Between the Two Kingdoms 49
   Ten Things Satan Wants for Your Life 51
   How To Resist Satan 57
   The Lord's Prayer 58
   Binding Evil Spirits That May Be Interfering in Your Life ... 59

The Three Realms..62
Discerning Strongholds in Your Life................................67
Deliverance...72
Deliverance Prayer in General..77
The Two Houses That Demons Can Occupy....................79
The Jezebel, Religious, and Antichrist Spirits....................80

Chapter 5. Hear God Speak 91

Dream Interpretation..94
Categories of dreams..101
Understanding the Many Faces of God in our Dreams...........106
Some of the Most Common Symbols in Dreams......................107
Understanding God's Messages..115
Two of My Dreams as Exercise...116

Chapter 6. The Rapture, Tribulation, And the Return of Christ............................119

The Rapture..120
The Tribulation..122
The Return of Jesus Christ..129
The Signs of Jesus Christ's Second Coming....................135

Conclusion..139
Prayer of Salvation 141
Final Quote...142
Dream Interpretation Symbols With Possible Meanings 143
Clothed For The King 166
Bibliography...168

Acknowledgements

I want to thank my husband, Marius Joubert, who always supports and encourages me in my assignments for God. We surely make a great team in helping to build the Kingdom of God.

Thank you to Ruth Zanetti and Danie Berndt for their valued advice as I prepared the book for publication.

Ellen Joubert

Foreword

My husband, our two daughters, and I immigrated from South Africa to Australia on the 16th of June 2006. This huge step was because my husband had a dream from God in 1998 to move to Australia. At the time, Marius was working as a linesman for South Africa's national power supplier. We lived on the grounds of a substation which consisted of thirteen houses, the main office building, and other workshop buildings. The area was known for heavy thunder and lightning storms during the summer season.

In the summer of 1998, Marius had the dream while working very hard. He was also busy with the final exam to complete his Electrical Engineering Diploma. There were continuous storms for two weeks, and he had to work from early in the morning till late at night to help repair power lines. Our children were babies, and we barely saw each other during those two weeks. I was struggling alone, looking after our small children, and Marius worked hard to supply our needs. After each hard working day, he also had to study from nine till midnight, or after.

Late one night, I took a relaxing bath after a busy day with our children. When Marius arrived home, he popped into the bathroom for a quick chat before going to study. He said he hoped not to wake up again at 5 am the following morning because he was exhausted. I asked what he meant. Although he was going to bed so late, he said, he woke up at 5 am for four consecutive mornings. I was doing a lot of Bible study during those days, and I suggested that maybe God was waking him up. If it happened again the following day, he should ask God if He had a message for him. The next day he did wake up at 5 am. He took his Bible and prayed: 'Lord, what would you like to say to me?' He could not read for longer than 5 minutes, and when he fell asleep, he dreamed that we should move to Australia. However, it took eight years before we emigrated.

When we left South Africa, we were on a spiritual high as we had walked an amazing path with the Lord for many years. We trusted in God's promises to us as we made the journey to Australia. The unknown was terrifying, but our trust in God was comforting.

Our arrival in Australia was a huge cultural shock, but the spiritual shock was debilitating. In South Africa, we could talk about God, Jesus Christ, and the Holy Spirit freely. In Australia, it was apparent that many people did not want to talk or hear about God. The name Jesus Christ was used as a curse word or in a joke. We soon realised it was best not to utter these words. Many people loved God in Australia, but this subject was taboo in many work environments.

At that time, I was working as an advertising executive in the newspaper industry. In full-time work, your colleagues are like your family because you see and interact with them for a large part of the day. Apart from a handful of people who were open to hearing my testimonies, most were not interested in hearing about Jesus Christ.

Towards the end of my career, I understood what it meant when the Bible says that creation will worship and praise God when His people do not want to. One day I was very sad and discouraged about how few people want to know about God. I asked Him why so many do not want to worship and praise Him. He opened the following Scripture to me about Jesus' last ride into Jerusalem, before His crucifixion:

Luke 19:37-40, *"As He (Jesus) was drawing near - already on the way down the Mount of Olives - the whole multitude of his disciples began to rejoice and praise God with a loud voice for all the mighty works that they had seen, saying, "Blessed is the King who comes in the name of the Lord! Peace in heaven and glory in the highest!" And some of the Pharisees (rulers of the Jews) in the crowd said to Him, "Teacher, rebuke your disciples." He answered, "I tell you, if these were silent, the very stones would cry out."*

My sadness disappeared when I decided to make sure that the stones would cry out. It was then that I began my *stone ministry*. Having a bag full of river stones at home, I started to paint Bible verses on them, and I placed them in strategic places around my yard and city. Verses to praise God, verses that bless the land, verses to break curses, and verses that acknowledge God for who He is. Throughout the Bible, many verses mention how all things on the earth and in heaven praise God. Many people on earth do not know or believe that Almighty God created them and do not accept or worship Him. Sadly they miss out on the great blessings that He wants to bestow on them. Most importantly, they will miss the gift of salvation and eternal life in heaven with Him.

Here are some Scriptures about how creation worships God:

- *"For you shall go out in joy and be led forth in peace; the mountains and the hills before you shall break forth into singing, and all the trees of the field shall clap their hands." - Isaiah 55:12 ESV.*

- *"For the stone will cry out from the wall, and the beam from the woodwork respond." - Habakkuk 2:11 ESV.*

- *"All the earth worships You and sings praises to You; they sing praises to Your name." - Psalm 66:4 ESV.*

- *"The heavens declare the glory of God, and the sky above proclaims His handiwork." - Psalm 19:1 ESV.*

- *"But ask the beasts, and they will teach you; the birds of the heavens, and they will tell you, or the bushes of the earth and they will teach you, and the fish of the sea will declare to you. Who among all these does not know that the hand of the Lord has done this? In His hand is the life of every living thing and the breath of all mankind." - Job 12:7-10 ESV.*

- *"The beast of the field will honour Me, the jackals and the ostriches, because I give waters in the wilderness and rivers in the desert, to give drink to My people, My chosen. These people I have formed for Myself, they shall declare My praise." - Isaiah 43:20-21 ESV.*

Worshipping God our Creator is the key to get to know Him better. In James 4:8 is the promise that if we draw near to Him, He will draw near to us. God wants us to be true worshippers that worship Him in Spirit and truth. External forms are not inconsistent, but they are not the essence. Firstly, God desires all people to be saved and come to know the truth (1 Timothy 2:4). Jesus is the way and the truth to the Father (John 14:6). To know Him is to love Him. We come to know God through the revelation of who He is (John 1:1-14). In John 4:23-24, Jesus said to the Samaritan woman, *"But the hour is coming, and now is, when the true worshippers will worship the Father in spirit and truth; for the Father is seeking such to worship Him. God is Spirit, and those who worship Him must worship in spirit and truth."*. Many people find it difficult to love God, and the reason is that they do not know Him.

When we consider God's creation and come to understand His work of salvation in Jesus Christ, we are in awe, lost in wonder, love, and praise (Psalm 33:6-9). True worship is a whole heart response to God's greatness and glory. In return, we give back to Him all that we are. Not just what we say, but how we live. We worship what we find most valuable. In Matthew 6:21, Jesus said: *"For where your treasure is, there your heart will also be"*. It is our expression of love, adoration, admiration, and gratitude for what God has done and still is doing for us. He has restored our relationship with Him, saved us from eternal death, and blesses us every day.

God has made the Gospel easy so that even a child can understand it! Jesus said to His disciples in Matthew 18:3, *"Assuredly, I say to you, unless you are converted and become as little children, you will by no means enter the kingdom of heaven."* The Gospel is the Good News of Jesus' birth, death and resurrection, which brought our salvation. The first four books of the New Testament are Matthew, Mark, Luke, John, and are known as The Gospels. These four disciples describe each in their own words what they experienced while moving with Jesus during His three and a half years of earthly ministry.

Why is it then that not everyone believes the message of the Gospel? The Bible states in 2 Corinthians 4:3-4 that the god of this world, Satan, has blinded the minds of unbelievers. In 1 Corinthians 2:14, we read that the unbeliever does not understand the things of God's Spirit and that it seems foolishness to them. God's Spirit or the Holy Spirit is the third person in what we know as the Trinity – Father *(God)*, Son *(Jesus)*, and Holy Spirit, who is always there for born-again believers. When we come to faith, we are born again by the Spirit of God. We are not saved by our good works but by what Jesus has accomplished. We receive salvation by faith. Good works follow from that. Our lives will then begin to manifest the fruits of the Holy Spirit – love, joy, peace, gentleness, kindness, patience, goodness, and self-control.

God wants us to have faith in Him. In Hebrew 11:1, Paul wrote, *"Now faith is the substance of things hoped for, the evidence of things not seen."* In Hebrew 11:6, he said, *"But without faith, it is impossible to please Him, for he who comes to God must believe that He is, and that He is a rewarder of those who diligently seek Him."* Also, please read the rest of Hebrew 11 to get the complete picture of how faith is illustrated. The Bible is full of stories of God's people who had faith in Him and who He blessed for being faithful. Let's take Noah's well-known story in Genesis 6-9, where God instructed him to build an ark. Noah had been divinely warned of things not yet seen, and by faith, he moved with godly fear to prepare an ark for the saving of his household and pairs of animals.

The apostle Paul also wrote, *"So then faith comes by hearing, and hearing by the Word of God"* (Romans 10:17). Therefore, the more we study the Bible and hear the words of God, the more truth will come forth, which will build our faith.

The Bible also teaches us that many people in the Church believing in Jesus Christ will not go to heaven. We cannot just accept Jesus as our Lord and Saviour and keep living in sin. Jesus' words in Matthew 7:21-23 are very clear on this when He said, *"Not everyone who says to Me, 'Lord, Lord,' will enter the kingdom of heaven, but the one who does the will of His Father who is in heaven. On that day (Judgment Day), many will say to Him, 'Lord, Lord, did we not prophesy in your name, and cast out demons in your name, and do many mighty works in your name?' And then He will declare to them, 'I never knew you; depart from me, you workers of lawlessness.'*

Judgement Day will come at the end of this present age when Jesus will judge the nations (Matthew 25:32). Accepting Jesus as our Lord and Saviour is the first step in receiving the gift of eternal life. He also wants us to manifest the fruits of the Spirit as described in Galatians 5:22-23. Jesus said He is the true vine, and His Father is the vinedresser. Every branch *(person)* in Him that does not bear fruit He'll take away; and every branch *(person)* that bears fruit, He prunes, that they may bear more fruit (John 15:1). The apostle Paul wrote in Romans 7:19-20, *"For I know that good itself does not dwell in me, that is, in my sinful nature. For I have the desire to do what is good, but I cannot carry it out. For I do not do the good, I want to do, but the evil I do not want to do - this I keep on doing."* Further on in this book, I'll explain what it means to be a born again Christian, and I'll go deeper into God's Word on how we should live after we have accepted Jesus Christ. I pray that the Holy Spirit will open the Scriptures for you.

I want to encourage you to start your own *Stone Ministry* as I did, wherever you are in the world. Let's soak this earth with stones that cry out the praises *(Scriptures)* to our God because He is a Good God and worthy to be praised! Let's break the curses on the land with the Word of God *(spiritual warfare scriptures)*. Chapter 4 explains how spiritual warfare works and how our struggles are not against flesh and blood *(people)*, but against the rulers, against the authorities, against the powers of this dark world, and the spiritual forces of evil in the heavenly realms *(evil spirits)*. In chapter 4, you'll also see how the Word of God is the strongest weapon used in spiritual warfare.

CHAPTER 1

WHY GOD LOVES US SO MUCH

God is our Father and knows when His children need a word of encouragement. Sometimes He has prompted me to tell someone that He loves them, and they have been deeply affected. God's nature is love, and we are created in His image. Therefore our spirit cries out to Him. Jesus came to fulfil God's plan of salvation so that we can be restored to fellowship with Him as in the beginning. Please read Genesis 3. God's perfect love is beyond our understanding. It is unconditional, and He wants us to come to Him as we are (1 John 4:9-10).

I once knew a couple who were having relationship issues. They were both headstrong. The man was an agnostic, and the woman was a Christian. He was upset because he felt that she loves God more than him. I explained that the love of God is spiritual, whereas love for a spouse, family and friends is different. Love for God is acknowledging who He is and being faithful to His commandments.

God demonstrates His love toward us in that while we were still sinners, Christ died for us (Romans 5:8). He draws us to Himself (John 6:44) because He is our Heavenly Father. He knows and loves each of us personally. He said to the prophet Jeremiah, *"Before I formed you in the womb I knew you"* King David wrote in Psalm 139:13 to God, *"For You created my inmost being; You knit me together in my mother's womb."* How wonderful to know that God knew each one of us before we came into existence! He wanted you and me to be born and be part of His family! Never listen to anyone telling you that you were a mistake. Even if your parents said they did not want you, God wanted you to be born. In Ephesians 1:4, we read, *"For He chose us in Him before the creation of the world to be holy and blameless in His sight."*

Earth was never meant to operate apart from heaven; it was meant to operate just like heaven. The rulership over the earth was given to Mankind (Genesis 1:27). When God created Adam and Eve, He placed them in His garden, and He said to them in Genesis 1:28, *"Be fruitful and increase in number; fill the earth and subdue it. Rule over the fish in the sea and the birds in the sky and over every living creature that moves on the earth."* God created Eve to be a helper suitable for Adam as He said it was not good for the man to be alone (Genesis 2:18).

The serpent *(devil)* deceived Eve in Genesis 3 by asking her: *"Did God really say, 'You must not eat from any tree in the garden'?"* and her answer was: *"We may eat fruit from the trees in the garden, but are not to eat any fruit from the tree that is in the middle of the garden; otherwise we'll die."* Then the serpent said to the woman, *"You will not surely die. For God knows that in the day you eat of it, your eyes will be opened, and you will be like God, knowing good and evil."*

When Eve saw that the fruit on the tree was good for food and pleasing to the eye, she took some and ate it. She also gave some to Adam, who was with her, and he ate. Eating the forbidden fruit was the fall of mankind, and we were stripped from our heavenly glory and authority. Nevertheless, God still loved us so much that He sent His only begotten Son, Jesus, to die on the cross to restore mankind's relationship with Him and redeem us from the curse of the law (Galatians 3:13).

God's love did not stop there! He inspired prophets, apostles, and anointed people to write the Bible books to guide us to know who He is and who we are in Christ. Some people say, 'But how can a *loving* God send people to hell?' I watched Christian television one day when I heard the following bold statement from a pastor: 'God does not send people to hell! People send themselves to hell!' This statement took me by surprise, as I didn't understand it at first.

Then I realised it is so true! With God's gift of eternal life, it is up to us to take it or reject it!

Following Christ Develops our Character

Many people say they are Christian, but how many are willing to follow Jesus Christ and do what He says? Jesus said in John 12:26, *"If anyone serves me, he must follow me; and where I am, there will my servant be also. If anyone serves me, the Father will honour him."*

When Jesus called the twelve disciples together, He gave them power and authority to drive out all demons and cure diseases. He sent them out to proclaim the kingdom of God and heal the sick. He told them: *"Take nothing for the journey, no staff, no bag, no bread, no money, no extra shirt. Whatever house you enter, stay there until you leave that town. If people do not welcome you, leave their town and shake the dust off your feet as a testimony against them."* (Luke 9:1-5). Apart from the twelve disciples who lived close to Jesus, He also chose seventy-two others and sent them ahead in pairs to all the towns and places He planned to visit (Luke 10:1).

A disciple was a dedicated follower or pupil of Christ during His life. In the ancient biblical world, disciples actively imitated both the life and teaching of their master. After Jesus ascended into heaven, His disciples became apostles, who were entrusted with spreading the Gospel and establishing the Church. Jesus said, *"Go into all the world and preach the Good News to everyone"* (Mark 16:15).

Once we understand and accept the Good News of Salvation through Jesus Christ, God commissioned us to spread the Gospel. In Matthew 28:18-20, Jesus said to His disciples: *"All authority in heaven and on earth has been given to me. Therefore go and make disciples of all nations, baptising them in the name of the Father and of the Son and the Holy Spirit, and teaching them to obey everything I have commanded you. And surely I am with you always, to the very end of the age."*

A faithful follower of Christ requires action and conversion. When we repent, we 'turn 180° and go God's way', e.g. not my way but Your way Lord. It is our unconditional surrender to God as Sovereign.

Following are a few Bible verses on repentance:

- *"Whoever conceals their sins does not prosper, but the one who confesses and renounces them finds mercy" (Proverbs 28:13).*

- *"Those whom I (Jesus) love I rebuke and discipline. So be earnest and repent" (Revelation 3:19).*

- *"For I take no pleasure in the death of anyone, declares the Sovereign Lord. Repent and live!" (Ezekiel 18:32).*

- *"The time has come, he (Paul) said. The kingdom of God has come near. Repent and believe the good news!" (Mark 1:15).*

- *"I (Jesus) tell you, no! But unless you repent, you too will all perish" (Luke 13:3).*

Jesus told His disciples in John 15:18-19, *"If the world hates you, keep in mind that it hated me first. If you belong to the world, it would love you as its own. As it is, you do not belong to the world, but I have chosen you out of the world."* Many Christians are hated and persecuted for Jesus Christ's name. Jesus also said to His disciples in John 16:33, *"In this world, you will have trouble. But take heart! I have overcome the world."* When Peter addressed the crowd in Acts 2, they asked, *"What shall we do?"* Peter replied, *"Repent and be baptised, every one of you, in the name of Jesus Christ for the forgiveness of your sins. And you will receive the gift of the Holy Spirit. The promise is for you and your children and for all who are far off - for all whom the Lord our God will call."*

A Christian character begins with faith in Christ, followed by choosing to behave God's way and not your way. God said in Hebrews 11:6 that without faith, it is impossible to please Him. People need to see Jesus's character in us. In difficult situations, we must always ask ourselves, 'What would Jesus do?' because we are ambassadors for Him.

Following are some great teachings from Jesus about character, taken from Matthew, Chapters 6 and 7:

- *Be careful not to practice your righteousness in front of others to be seen by them.*

- *When helping the needy, do not announce it with trumpets, as the synagogues' hypocrites do. Or on the streets, to be honoured by others. Those have received their reward in full. But when you give to the needy, do not let your left hand know what your right hand is doing, so that your giving may be in secret. Then your Father, who sees what's done in secret, will reward you.*

- *When you pray, do not be like the hypocrites. They love to stand in the synagogues and on the street corners to be seen by others. They have received their reward in full. But when you pray, go into your room, close the door and pray to your unseen Father. Then your Father, who sees what is done in secret, will reward you.*

- *When you pray, do not keep on babbling like pagans. They think with many words, God will hear their prayers. Do not be like them, for your Father knows what you need before you ask him.*

- *Forgive other people when they sin against you, then your heavenly Father will also forgive you. If you do not forgive others their sins, your Father will not forgive your sins.*

- *When you are fasting, do not look sombre as the hypocrites do, for they disfigure their faces to show others they are fasting. They have received their reward in full. But when you fast, put oil on your head and wash your face, so that it will not be evident to others that you are fasting, but only to your unseen Father, who sees what's done in secret, and He'll reward you.*

- *Do not store up for yourselves treasures on earth, where moths and vermin destroy, and where thieves break in and steal. Store up for yourselves treasures in heaven, where moths and vermin do not destroy, and where thieves do not break in and steal. For where your treasure is, there your heart will also be.*

- *The eye is the lamp of the body. If your eyes are healthy, your whole body will be full of light. But if your eyes are unhealthy, your entire body will be full of darkness.*

- *No one can serve two masters. Either you will hate the one and love the other, or you will be devoted to the one and despise the other. You cannot serve both God and money.*

- *Do not worry about your life, what you will eat or drink, or about your body, what you will wear. Is not life more than food, and the body more than clothes? Look at the birds of the air; they do not sow or reap or store away in barns, and yet your heavenly Father feeds them. Are you not much more valuable than they?*

- *Do not judge, or you too will be judged. For in the same way you judge others, you'll be judged. With the measure you use, you'll be measured. Why do you look at the speck of sawdust in your brother's eye and pay no attention to the plank in your eye? You hypocrite, first take the plank out of your eye, and then you will see clearly to remove the speck from your brother's eye.'*

- *Do not give dogs what is sacred; do not throw your pearls to pigs. If you do, they may trample them under their feet and turn and tear you to pieces.*

- *Ask, and you'll receive; seek, and you will find; knock, and the door will be opened to you. For everyone who asks receives; the one who seeks finds; and to the one who knocks, the door will be opened.*

- *Watch out for false prophets. They come to you in sheep's clothing, but inwardly they are ferocious wolves. By their fruit, you will recognise them.*

- *Not everyone who says to Jesus, 'Lord, Lord,' will enter the kingdom of heaven, but only the ones who do the will of God the Father, who is in heaven.*

- *In the end, Jesus said: Everyone who hears these words of mine and puts them into practice is like a wise man who built his house on the rock. The rain came down, the streams rose, and the winds blew and beat against that house, yet it did not fall, because it had its foundation on the rock. But everyone who hears these words of mine and does not put them into practice is like a foolish man who built his house on sand. The rain came down, the streams rose, and the winds blew and beat against that house, and it fell with a great crash.*

Jesus always spoke the truth, so a follower of Christ should also speak the truth at all times! In John 8:44, Jesus said to those who do not have truth in them, *"You belong to your father, the devil, and you want to carry out your father's desires. He was a murderer from the beginning, not holding to the truth, for there is no truth in him. When he lies, he speaks his native language, for he is a liar and the father of lies."*

By living in truth, the devil cannot get a foothold in our life. Being a Christian does not shelter us from trials and sufferings. Paul wrote in Romans 5:3-5 that we must rejoice in our suffering, knowing that suffering produces endurance, endurance produces character, and character produces hope. Knowledge of God through reading the Bible and prayer builds a Christ-like character in us.

Choose your friends with caution. Paul warns us in 1 Corinthians 15:33, *"Bad company ruins good morals",* and in Romans 12:2 he said, *"And do not be conformed to this world, but be transformed by the renewing of your mind, that you may prove what is that good and acceptable and perfect will of God".*

In Christ, we receive the Holy Spirit, who is there to help us grow a Christian character so that we are not alone in trying to be like Christ. From the point where we repent and give our lives to the Lord, it is a step-by-step walk to get closer to the character God expects of us. It's a process and not an overnight change. The closer our daily walk is with the Lord, the more people will see the nature of Christ manifest in us. Our character begins to develop the fruit of the Holy Spirit in us, such as love, joy, peace, patience, kindness, goodness, faithfulness, gentleness, self-control (Galatians 5:22-23).

The Meaning of Being Born Again

Being born again means accepting Christ and giving up your old life to live a new life through Christ Jesus. In 2 Corinthians 5:17, apostle Paul said, *"Therefore if any man is in Christ, he is a new creature: old things are passed away; behold, all things become new."* It may sound complicated, but it is the work of the Holy Spirit in us. Unless a person is born again, they cannot see the kingdom of God. That is why Jesus sent the Holy Spirit as another one like Him, who comes alongside us.

Jesus taught a Pharisee named Nicodemus, a member of the Jewish ruling council, about being born again in John 3. Nicodemus came to Jesus at night and said, *"Rabbi, we know that you are a teacher who has come from God. For no one could perform the signs you are doing if God were not with him."* Jesus replied, *"Most assuredly, I say to you, unless one is born again, he cannot see the kingdom of God."* Nicodemus answered, *"How can a man be born when he is old? He cannot enter a second time into his mother's womb and be born, can he?"*

Jesus answered, *"Very truly I tell you, no one can enter the kingdom of God unless they are born of water and the Spirit. Flesh gives birth to flesh, but the Spirit (Holy Spirit) gives birth to spirit. You should not be surprised at my saying, 'You must be born again.' The wind blows wherever it pleases. You hear its sound, but you cannot tell where it comes from or where it is going. So it is with everyone born of the Spirit."* But Nicodemus still did not understand what Jesus was saying and asked again, *"How can this be?"*

Jesus explained again to Nicodemus in John 3:10-18, *"You are Israel's teacher, and do you not understand these things? Very truly I tell you, we speak of what we know, and we testify to what we have seen, but still you people do not accept our testimony."* Jesus continued, *"I have spoken to you of earthly things, and you do not believe; how then will you believe if I speak of heavenly things? No man has ever gone into heaven except the one who came from heaven, the Son of Man (Jesus). Just as Moses lifted up the snake in the wilderness, so the Son of Man must be lifted up, that everyone who believes may have eternal life in Him. God so loved the world that he gave His one and only Son that whoever believes in Him shall not perish but have eternal life. For God did not send his Son into the world to condemn the world, but to save the world through Him. Whoever believes in Him is not condemned, but whoever does not believe stands condemned already because they have not believed in the name of God's one and only Son."*

To be born again is a spiritual rebirth. The Holy Spirit comes into our spirit when we believe in Christ our Lord and Saviour. Ephesians 1:13 says, *"And you also were included in Christ when you heard the message of truth, the Gospel of your salvation. When you believed, you were marked in Him with a seal, the promised Holy Spirit."* In this context, Merriam-Webster defines 'believe' to have a firm or wholehearted religious conviction or persuasion: to regard the existence of God as a fact.

In Acts Chapter 1, when Jesus was eating with His disciples, after His resurrection, He said to them, *"Do not leave Jerusalem but wait for the gift (Holy Spirit) my Father promised, which you have heard me speak about. For John baptised with water, but in a few days you will be baptised with the Holy Spirit."* (Acts 1:4-5). The Holy Spirit did not come until Jesus ascended into heaven. Now that Jesus is in heaven, the Holy Spirit comes immediately after a person repents of their sins and professes Jesus Christ as their Lord and Saviour. A person may not feel a change or hear the Holy Spirit immediately, but will in time as they grow in grace and the knowledge of God (2 Peter 3:18).

In 2 Timothy 1:14, Paul says, *"Guard the good deposit that was entrusted to you, guard it with the help of the Holy Spirit who lives in us."* In Romans 8:9, he wrote, *"You, however, are not in the flesh but in the Spirit, if in fact, the Spirit of God dwells in you. Anyone who does not have the Spirit of Christ does not belong to Him."* 2 Corinthians 1:21-22 read, *"Now it is God who makes both us and you stand firm in Christ. He anointed us, set his **seal of ownership** on us, and put his Spirit in our hearts as a deposit, guaranteeing what is to come."* **Romans 8:16** also says, *"The Spirit himself bears witness with our spirit that we are children of God."* Jesus sent us the Holy Spirit to do what He would do if He had remained with us.

As I was writing this born again section, I heard an Evangelist teaching on the subject. He said that there are secret societies against Christ, who also uses the term 'born again'. People need to partake in unethical and ungodly ways to become a member of the secret society. They call these ungodly actions being born again. For example, a particular secret society expects the new member to sleep in a coffin, and when they wake up, they would supposedly be born again. There are many more weird things new members have to do. This act is not the 'born again' that Jesus teaches us about in the Bible! Satan started these secret societies to hijack Jesus's teaching and lead people astray.

The Blood Sacrifice

Why was a blood sacrifice needed to wash away our sins? The Bible regards blood as the symbol and source of life. Leviticus 17:14 states, *"For the life of every creature is its blood: its blood is its life...."*

In the Old Testament:

- God required animal sacrifices as a way for His people to atone for their sins and draw nearer to Him temporarily. Once a year, they had to bring unblemished animals to the Priest to be sacrificed for the atonement of their sins (Leviticus 16:34). This was called the Day of Atonement. Unblemished means to have no flaws or marks. This blood sacrifice in the Old Testament foreshadowed the coming of Jesus and His death upon the cross to redeem the world.

In the New Testament:

- Only Jesus could be sacrificed for the atonement of all the sins of humankind because He was sinless. In Hebrews 9:22, Paul said, *"Indeed, under the law, almost everything is purified with blood, and without the shedding of blood, there is no forgiveness of sins."*

- Jesus's blood paid for our sins, **once** for all (Romans 6:9-10). Hebrews 9:12 reads, *"Not with the blood of goats and calves, but with His own blood He entered the Most Holy Place **once** for all, having obtained eternal redemption."* Therefore there is no need for any sacrifice anymore because Jesus has done it ONCE FOR ALL. His last words on the cross before He bowed His head and gave up His spirit was: *"It is finished" – John 19:30.*

In Timothy 2:3-4, the apostle Paul wrote that God desires all men to be saved and come to know the truth. The apostle Peter wrote in 2 Peter 3:9, *"The Lord is not slow in keeping His promise, as some understand slowness. Instead, He is patient with you, not wanting anyone to perish, but everyone to come to repentance."*

Mankind was made in God's image but are not God; therefore, the possibility was always there that mankind would fall. But since the beginning, God had a plan to reconcile all things to himself (Colossians 1:20). We were all created with free will because God wanted us to love Him freely. He did not want robots. The apostle John said in 1 John 5:3 that love for God is that we keep His commandments, and His commandments are not burdensome.

In a prayer of repentance after committing adultery with Bathsheba (2 Samuel 11), David cried out to God to be washed and cleansed of his sin (Psalm 51:7). Those who were unclean were not allowed to enter into the presence of a Holy God. Adam and Eve's sin in eating the forbidden fruit made them unclean and separated them from God. By accepting Jesus, we are made clean through His shed blood, which allows us to communicate with God our Father again. Jesus said, *"I am the way, the truth, and the life. No one comes to the Father except through Me"* (John 14:6).

If you would like to accept Jesus Christ as your Lord and Saviour, pray the following prayer. If no one is there to pray with you, just come as you are. Ask the Holy Spirit to bear witness to your prayer and then tell someone what you have done.

PRAYER OF REPENTANCE

Dear God, I am a sinner! Thank you that Jesus died for me on the Cross of Calvary.
Please forgive me for all my sins which I have committed against You my Father in Heaven, and the sins I have committed against Jesus Christ my Lord and Saviour, and the sins I have committed against the Holy Spirit. Please wash and cleanse me in the Blood of Jesus Christ, Your Son, my Saviour.

Come and live in my heart; I make you my Lord and Saviour. I want to be guided by You and taught in all the truths of Your Word by the Holy Spirit.

Make me strong, and keep me on the straight and narrow path so that I can make my eternal home with You. I am looking forward to the day I'll be united with You.

I pray this in the Name of Jesus Christ.

Amen and Amen!

CHAPTER 2

IS GOD REAL AND IS THE BIBLE RELIABLE?

In this chapter, I would like to discuss the views of some scholars on the subject of science. I've heard people say that Christians made up the story about God, and Jesus Christ, to make them feel better. The field of science is such a challenging subject that only those who study it can understand it. For the average person, the terminology and reasoning behind it can be confusing.

I have heard scientists who believe in God and those who do not. Both can sound very convincing. Each one had all their facts together, and it was easy to believe in their point of view. It's so easy for ordinary people to believe everything scientists tell us. We think they know better than us, and they usually sound like geniuses. Just as I encourage people to study the Word of God themselves and not just believe every preacher or person's teaching on it, I also want to encourage you to research science to make sure that what they say is the truth.

When I started my walk with God, I had many questions. There were times when my husband explained something about the Bible to me, and when I was not entirely convinced, I said to him, 'prove it to me from the Bible, and I'll believe you'. We still joke about it today, but this is how we should be. Do not believe just anyone until they can prove what they say is true. Understanding God's Word is a matter of life and death. It's the difference between eternal life or eternal death.

Of course, we would never understand the whole Bible on our own because our life on earth is too short. That is why God instructs the body of Christ to build each other up. The body of Christ is every believer. In Ephesians 4:14-16, we read: *"Then we will no longer be infants, tossed back and forth by the waves, and blown here and there by every wind of teaching and by the cunning and craftiness of people in their deceitful scheming. Instead, speaking the truth in love, we will grow to become in every respect the mature body of him who is the head, that is, Christ. From Him, the whole body joined and held together by every supporting ligament, grows and builds itself up in love, as each part does its work."*

Believers receive different gifts from God, and together we form the body of Christ. Therefore, we need each other to become more like Him. In 1 Corinthians 12:12-31, Paul writes to the Church, *"For just as the body is one and has many members, and all the members of the body, though many, are one body, so it is with Christ. For in one Spirit, we were all baptised into one body, Jews or Greeks, slaves or free, and all were made to drink of one Spirit. For the body does not consist of one member but many. If the foot should say, 'Because I am not a hand, I do not belong to the body,' that would not make it any less a part of the body. And if the ear should say, 'Because I am not an eye, I do not belong to the body,' that would not make it any less a part of the body...."*

The Bible

In 2018, I heard one of Dr David Jeremiah's sermons on Christian television about the Bible. This teaching was so outstanding that I decided to find it on YouTube to listen to the facts about the Bible again as he gave them. He mentioned that a few years ago, he saw an article in the *New Yorker Magazine* about 'The Good Book Business' and why publishers love the Bible. The writer made a remarkable claim that the Bible is the best selling book of all time. An even more remarkable claim was that the Bible is the *Best Selling Book of the Year* every year! In the United States alone, fifty Bibles are sold every minute, seventy-two thousand every day, and twenty-six million every year. By comparison, the top five best booksellers combined sold twelve million copies. The total number of Bibles printed and distributed since they took note of it is between six and seven billion. In comparison, the three best-selling single volumes of all time are *A Tale of Two Cities* which sold two-hundred million; *The Lord of the Rings*, which sold hundred-and-fifty million; and *The Little Prince*, which sold hundred-and-forty million copies.

The *Gideons* alone, during their one hundred years of ministry, distributed 1.6 Billion copies of the Bible in more than hundred-and-ninety countries around the world. They are just one of many entities committed to the worldwide distribution of the Bible. Hundreds of publishers, thousands of outlets, and millions of people share the good news of Jesus Christ, as revealed in the Bible. More people read the Bible than any other book. Without question, it is the most important book in the world! And it is read not only by Christian believers but also politicians, royalty, and renowned intellectuals. For example, Sir Winston Churchill called the Bible a masterpiece. Writers as diverse as Milton, Swift, Scott, and Shakespeare have borrowed liberally from its pages. If you would delete every Biblical reference from the great art and literature of the world, our galleries and libraries would shrink. Artists, poets, writers, sculptures, and musicians; have filled the world with their works based on biblical themes. No book in the history of the world has inspired more creativity than the Bible.

The Bible was written over a span of fifteen hundred years by more than forty authors who came from all walks of life. They were farmers, historians, fishermen, kings, prophets, and apostles. It was written in three languages: Hebrew, Aramaic, and Greek, and in four Geopolitical Regions: The Middle East, Mesopotamia, Asia Minor, and Southern Europe. The Holy Spirit of God moved the writers of Scripture, as they wrote so that the words they recorded were nothing less than the very words of God but written in their style.

John Wycliffe completed the first English translation of the Bible in 1382, A.D. It was first printed in 1454 A.D. by Johannes Gutenberg, who invented the first mechanical moveable type printing press. The Bible was the first book he ever printed. History shows that the development of European culture was based upon the Bible. The Ten Commandments are the cornerstone of our jurisprudence. It also forms the foundation of all morality and ethics in western civilization. Many sayings people use every day come from the Bible, for example, "the signs of the times", "the spirit is willing, but the flesh is weak", "eat drink and be merry", "saved by the skin of your teeth", and many more! Even many leadership and management methods include principles taken from the Bible.

Thousands of ancient manuscripts show by comparison with modern translations that the Bible we read today is unchanged, even though translated from another language. There are minor variations, but none to alter the fundamentals of Christian belief. Archaeology confirms more as time goes by regarding the authenticity of the Bible.

Dr Hugh Ross from Canada is a scientist and a Bible scholar. He got his PhD from the University of Toronto. I looked at one of his clips on *Mythbusters: God and Science*. At the age of seven, he started to study astronomy. From the age of eight, he knew that astrophysics would be his career. Every year after that, he looked at a different subdiscipline of astronomy. By the age of sixteen, he dedicated a whole year to study cosmology, which is the science of the origin, structure, and history of the universe. Dr Ross said that even then, there was a massive debate about whether we live in an oscillating universe as the Hindus teach, or a steady-state universe as in Buddhism, a hesitating universe, or is it a Big Bang Universe? Back in the 1960s, the astronomical evidence favoured the Big Bang Theory. If there was a big bang, there was a beginning. If there was a beginning, there must be a Beginner. From the age of sixteen, he did not doubt God's existence, but he was very sceptical that this God, who created fifty billion trillion stars, would want to communicate in a serious way with these beings on a little speck called planet earth. He began to look at the great philosophers to see if this God who created the universe was indeed communicating with us. He then started to read books by Immanuel Kant, who is the father of modern-day cosmology. Kant wrote a lot about God and the universe. Dr Ross discovered in his writings that he believed that space and time are eternal, but already there was evidence that it was not. After that, he read several other philosophers but decided to look at the world's great religions as well.

He found that Hinduism has books called the Vedas. There is quite a bit in these about astronomy, but they teach that the universe has multiple beginnings. Where there is a beginning, the universe collapses, then it starts again. The Vedas state that there are 4.32 billion years between one beginning of the universe and the next beginning. At the age of seventeen, Dr Ross knew that this was not correct. He also knew that the universe had an entropy measure *(a measure of uncertainty or randomness)* that was a hundred million times too high to permit any rebound of the universe. Therefore he had to put Hinduism aside. He then looked at the Buddhist commentaries and found that they borrowed their material about the universe from Hinduism. Therefore, he also set aside Buddhism. After that, he looked at the Quran of Islam, which has three different texts that deal with creation, but they contradict one another. One of them says that the stars are closer to us than the planets, but even with the naked eye, one can tell that the planets must be much closer to us than the stars. The Greeks figured that out. They determined that the stars had to be bodies just like the sun because they could not measure parallax with the naked eye *(the apparent movement of objects when viewed from different positions)*. Dr Ross said further that he found several other issues. For example, the Quran tells us that the human female's gestation period is six months, but women know it's nine months.

Finally, he took up a Bible. He didn't meet any Christians till he was 27 years of age, which happened when he joined Caltech. When he arrived there, he was stunned by how many of the most famous astronomers were followers of Jesus Christ. They helped Dr Ross launch his book *Reasons to Believe*.

At the age of eleven, he had received a *Gideon New Testament* at school but only started to read it when he was seventeen. Right away, he noticed how different it was. It wasn't vague, it wasn't esoteric, it wasn't repetitious like you see in other holy books. The Bible was clear, direct, and specific. It gave names and dates; talked about geography, history, and science. He then said to himself, this is a book that he could put to the test without a whole lot of trouble.

In 1 Thessalonians 5:21, he read, *"Test everything. Hold on to the good"*. What impressed Dr Ross as a seventeen-year-old was that the Bible not only encouraged him to put everything to the test, it showed him step-by-step how to do it. He was taught the scientific method at school, but none of his public teachers told him where this scientific method came from. After he picked up his *Gideon New Testament,* he found it on the first page. He also found it in every significant creation text in the Bible. He now calls it the 'Biblical Testing Method'.

It is no accident that the scientific revolution exploded out of reformation Europe when ordinary people could read the Bible for themselves. Scientists then discovered this testing method in the Bible and applied it to their scientific endeavours, which led to the scientific revolution. I encourage you to read some of Dr Hugh Ross' books on how he proved that the Bible is the inspired Word of God and how it interlinks with science.

Many people are ignorant of the fact that the Bible contains God's own words. If these two brilliant teachers' facts did not inspire you, and you still have doubts, I urge you to do proper research. Ask the Holy Spirit to guide you to the correct answers. I have done my research over almost three decades, and I do not doubt that the Bible contains God's very own words that teach us how to overcome adversity, having confidence in God who loves us and only wants the best for our lives. It starts with knowledge of the Bible! *"Through knowledge, we build our confidence, and with confidence, we overcome all the devil's lies!" (Quote from my book: Clothed for the King).*

Five Reasons that Affirm the Bible

Adrian Rogers, an American pastor and evangelist, gives five reasons to affirm that the Bible is the Word of God:

Firstly, because of its scientific accuracy. In Job 26:7, Job said, *"He stretcheth out the north over the empty place, and hangeth the earth upon nothing."* How did Job know that the earth hung in space before the age of modern astronomy and space travel? The Holy Spirit told him! Even in Isaiah's day, scientists didn't know the topography of the earth, but he wrote in Isaiah 40:20, *"It is He (God) that sitteth upon the circle of the earth."* The word 'circle' here refers to a globe or sphere. How did Isaiah know that God sits upon the sphere of the earth? Other than by divine inspiration of the Holy Spirit?

Secondly, through historical accuracy. For example, in the book of Daniel, Chapter 5, King Belshazzar hosted a great feast with thousands of his lords. Suddenly, a ghostly hand appeared and began to write on a wall. The king was very disturbed and called for the astrologers, the Chaldeans, and the soothsayers. He said whosoever could interpret the writing, be clothed with purple, have a chain of gold around his neck, and be the third ruler in the kingdom. All the king's wise men could not interpret the writing on the wall.

Then the queen said to the king, *'Do not let thy thoughts trouble thee. There is a man in thy kingdom, in whom is the spirit of the holy gods. Thy father, king Nebuchadnezzar called him Belteshazzar. He has a keen mind and knowledge and understanding, and the ability to interpret dreams, explain riddles and solve difficult problems. Call for Daniel, and he will tell you what the writing means".* After Daniel's interpretation, King Belshazzar commanded that he be clothed in purple, that a gold chain is placed around his neck, and it was proclaimed that he would be the third-highest ruler in the kingdom (Daniel 5:29).

Basing their opinion on Babylonian records, some historians claim this never happened. According to the documents, the last king of Babylon was not Belshazzar but a man named Nabonidus. And so, they said, the Bible is in error. There wasn't a record of a king named Belshazzar. Archaeologists continued to do their work, and in 1853, an inscription was found on a cornerstone of a temple built by Nabonidus to the god Ur, which read, *"May I, Nabonidus, king of Babylon, not sin against thee. And may reverence for thee dwell in the heart of Belshazzar, my first-born favourite son."* From other inscriptions, it was learned that Belshazzar and Nabonidus were joint rulers. Nabonidus travelled while Belshazzar stayed home to run the kingdom. Now that we know that Belshazzar and Nabonidus were joint rulers, it makes sense that Belshazzar would say that Daniel would be the third-highest ruler.

Thirdly, from Genesis to Revelation, the Bible reads as one book. It's made up of sixty-six books, written by forty different authors, yet there is incredible unity to it. The Bible forms one beautiful temple of truth that does not contradict itself theologically, morally, ethically, doctrinally, scientifically, historically, or in any other way.

Fourthly, the Bible is the only book in the world that has accurate prophecy! When you read the prophecies of the Bible, you simply have to stand back in awe. Over three hundred precise prophecies about the Lord Jesus Christ in the Old Testament are fulfilled in the New Testament. To say that they are fulfilled by chance is absurd.

Fifthly, the Bible is not a book of the month but the book of the ages. First Peter 1:25 says, *"But the Word of the Lord endureth forever. And this is the Word which by the Gospel was preached unto you."* No book has ever had as much opposition as the Bible. Men have laughed at it, scorned it, burned it, ridiculed it, and made laws against it, but the Word of God has survived over all the centuries. It is applicable today as much as it was yesterday and will be tomorrow. It is so profound that scholars will never plumb its depths, yet so simple that a little child can understand its message.

CHAPTER 3

THE ENEMIES OF MAN & THE ENEMIES OF GOD

The Enemies of Man

From the time that Satan persuaded Eve to eat the forbidden fruit, Satan and his demons have been the enemies of humanity (Genesis 3). Satan and his demons work through people to deceive, persecute, and kill the followers of Christ. Even our own families, and friends, can be used to mislead and lie to us. Therefore we must use our knowledge of the Bible and spiritual warfare to protect ourselves. Through prayer and Bible study, we build our confidence in Christ. We read in Ephesians 6:11, *"Put on the full armour of God so that you will be able to stand firm against the schemes of the devil."*

The Enemies of God

An enemy of God is someone who opposes the presence and purposes of God. The Bible identifies Satan, the devil, as the enemy of God (Matthew 16:23, Revelation 13:6), and he has many evil angels *(demons)* assisting him. These enemies work through humans who give them authority in their lives, just like Eve did in the Garden of Eden. Satan and his demons can't hurt or overcome Almighty God. Still, they hurt God indirectly by causing His people to be rebellious against Him and hurting them physically, mentally, and financially.

It is very hurtful to God to see His people perish because they are unsaved. Romans 10:9 says, *"If you confess with your mouth that Jesus is Lord and believe in your heart that God raised him from the dead, you will be saved."* An unsaved person is spiritually dead and lost as he travels with the crowd on the broad road to eternal torment. To be lost means not redeemed through Christ. Friendship with the world makes us an enemy of God. Some people may be religious, claiming to be believers, and do various religious things, but they do not have a personal relationship with God. They want to continue with the pleasures the world offers and want to control their own lives. In Revelation 3:45, God says, *"I know your deeds, that you are neither cold nor hot. I wish you were either one or the other! So, because you are lukewarm, neither hot nor cold, I am about to spit you out of my mouth."*

Thank God for Godly people who continually pray for their family. Although many people aren't saved yet, there may have been grandparents or parents who prayed for them. God honours the prayers of Godly people. He keeps working on the hearts of the unsaved so that they repent and be saved. So keep praying for your unsaved family and friends, and see how God honours your prayers! In James 5:16, we read that the prayer of a righteous person is powerful and effective.

Many people accept God, Jesus, and the Holy Spirit when they hear the Gospel, but others will listen to it again-and-again, and still harden their hearts, denying God's existence. These people deliberately reject God for different reasons. Some say seeing is believing. They want to see God first before they believe in Him. In Hebrews 11:1, Paul says faith is the substance of things hoped for, the evidence of things not seen. In verse six, he said that ***it is impossible to please God without faith***. Anyone who comes to Him must believe that He exists and rewards those who earnestly seek him. In 1 Peter 1:8-9, we also read, *"Though you have not seen Him, you love Him; and even though you do not see Him now, you believe in Him and are filled with an* *inexpressible and glorious joy, for you are receiving the end result of your faith, the salvation of your souls."*

Some sceptics say, 'show me a miracle, and I'll believe'. Even if they see genuine miracles, they would still doubt it or look for a naturalistic explanation. They keep finding other reasons to continue in their unbelief. Others, again, do not want to commit to God, their Creator, because of their worldview. They are confused and would instead study other religions than studying the Bible.

Others enjoy the world's pleasures and do not want to follow any rules but want to do what they want. The Bible describes running after all the world's pleasures as adultery against God, which means to rebel against Him and His laws. By rejecting Almighty God, believing in man-made gods, or no God, a person becomes adulterous to the One True Triune God (God the Father, God the Son, and God the Holy Spirit). These adulterous people then become enemies of God. James 4:4 explains this, *"You adulterous people, don't you know that friendship with the world means enmity against God? Therefore, anyone who chooses to be a friend of the world becomes an enemy of God."*

In Romans 1:18-25, the apostle Paul describes God's wrath against sinful humanity: *"[18] The wrath of God is being revealed from heaven against all the godlessness and wickedness of people, who suppress the truth by their wickedness, [19] since what may be known about God is plain to them because God has made it plain to them. [20] For since the creation of the world, God's invisible qualities, His eternal power and divine nature have been clearly seen, being understood from what has been made, so that people are without excuse. [21] For although they knew God, they neither glorified Him as God nor gave thanks to Him, but their thinking became futile, and their foolish hearts were darkened. [22] Although they claimed to be wise, they became fools [23] and exchanged the glory of the immortal God for images made to look like a mortal human being and birds and animals and reptiles. [24] Therefore God gave them over in the sinful desires of their hearts to sexual impurity for the degrading of their bodies with one another. [25] They exchanged the truth about God for a lie, and worshipped and served created things rather than the Creator who is forever praised. Amen."*

Through verse nineteen in the above passage, it is clear that there is no excuse for not believing in Almighty God. There is nothing complicated about the message of Jesus. The only requirements are to accept it and to believe.

For those who say they want to see the Glory of God first before they believe, I want to quote the following Scripture. After Jesus raised Lazarus from the dead in John 11, He said to Martha in verse 40, *"Did I not tell you that if you believe, you will see the glory of God?"* Therefore, the simple lesson here is that we have to believe in Almighty God first before we'll see His Glory.

Satan and his followers propagate a misconception that 'All religions pray to the same God'. Satan is working very hard to persuade religions to unite to create a 'One World Religion'. Let's turn to Aristotle's law of non-contradiction in consideration of the validity of universal salvation. This law states that opposite truth claims cannot both be valid, and it remains instructive as we explore the argument that all religions are different paths to the same God. The reality is that every religion makes absolute truth claims about God. Let's take the five major religions in the world: *Christians* declare that God is a Trinitarian communion of Father, Son, and the Holy Spirit. *Judaism* believes in one God who revealed himself through the ancient prophets. *Islam* holds that God is simply one and has no son. *Hinduism* acknowledges millions of deities, while *Buddhism* seems to be without a belief in a personal God.

In terms of logic, it can be affirmed that the validity of this diversity of absolute truth claims about God is from a subjective point of view. There is no reason to doubt the earnestness of the beliefs held by the faithful of each religion. However, the law of non-contradiction seems to rule out the possibility that each religion's understanding of God is equally valid and accurate from an objective point of view. It would seem to suggest that all religions do not ultimately lead to the same God since all do not believe in the same God.

In Biblical times, Saul of Tarsus was a child of the best upbringing, a student of the great Jewish teacher, Gamaliel. He was a Roman citizen, trained in the best schools. Groomed, perhaps, to even become a chief priest. This pious man who was zealous for

God was bent on destroying the believers in Jesus Christ. Only a few short years had passed from the crucifixion and resurrection of Jesus when this self-righteous religious zealot assisted in the murder by stoning one of Christianity's earliest martyrs named Stephen, who by his death bears witness to the Gospel. In Acts 8:1, Luke writes, *"Now Saul was consenting to his death"*, but even before that fateful day when young Saul the Pharisee gloated over the brutal death of the innocent disciple Stephen, the Spirit of Christ was pricking his heart. After the death of Stephen, Saul was passionate about destroying this new sect. He launched a holy war against the Church, scattering the believers. He created havoc, entering homes and sending many to prison, even putting some to death.

When word came that these followers of Jesus had spread into Syria, he requested permission to go to Damascus. With great delight, the High Priest granted him letters to take to the synagogues of Syria. As Saul and his colleagues came near Damascus, suddenly, they were flooded with a *glorious light*. Saul fell to the ground as a voice spoke from within the light. It was both terrifying and soothing at the same time, saying, *"Saul, Saul, why are you persecuting me?"* Saul inquired, *"Who are you, Lord?"* and the voice said, *"I am Jesus, whom you are persecuting."* Then Jesus said, *"Now get up and stand on your feet. I have appeared to you to appoint you as a servant and as a witness of what you have seen and will see of me. I will rescue you from your own people and from the Gentiles. I am sending you to them to open their eyes and turn them from darkness to light, and from the power of Satan to God, so that they may receive forgiveness of sins and a place among those who are sanctified by faith in me."* (Acts 26:14-18).

Acts 9 records the conversion of Saul, later Paul, from an unbeliever to a believer. He was born again and made a hundred-and-eighty degree turnaround to become a passionate follower of Christ. Through the divine revelation of the Holy Spirit, he wrote one-third of the New Testament. In 1 Corinthians 8:5-6, he wrote to the Church, *"For although there may be so-called gods in heaven or on earth, as indeed there are many 'gods' and many 'lords', yet for us there is one God, the Father, from whom are all things and for whom we exist, and one Lord, Jesus Christ, through whom are all things and through whom we exist."*

In Galatians 1:6-10, he wrote, *"I am astonished that you are so quickly deserting Him who called you in the grace of Christ and are turning to a different gospel, not that there is another one, but there are some who trouble you and want to distort the Gospel of Christ. But even if we or an angel from heaven should preach to you a gospel contrary to the one we preached to you, let him be accursed. As we have said before, so now I say again: If anyone is preaching to you a gospel contrary to the one you received, let him be accursed. For am I now seeking the approval of man, or of God? Or am I trying to please man? If I were still trying to please man, I would not be a servant of Christ."*

What a great testimony of the apostle Paul! Over the centuries, there were other conversions similar to Paul's, documented in books, videos, and television, who became followers of Christ because He showed himself to them. He is not dead! He is still alive and working towards saving people by appearing to them personally.

God is Light

There are so many Scriptures in the Bible that refer to God as light. 1 John 1:5, we read, *"God is Light, and in Him, there is no darkness at all."* Other Scriptures confirming that God is light are Habakkuk 3:4, Psalm 44:3, Psalm 50:2, Psalm 94:1, 2 Samuel 22:13, Hosea 6:5, Matthew 28:3. In the beginning, when the earth and everything in it was created, *He* who is *Light* said, *"Let there be light"* (Genesis 1:3). Paul wrote in 2 Corinthians 4:6-7, *"For God, who said, "Let light shine out of darkness," made His light shine in our hearts to give us the light of the knowledge of God's glory displayed in the face of Christ. But we have this treasure in jars of clay to show that this all-surpassing power is from God and not from us."*

Following is an excellent teaching I received from The Evangelist and Pastor John Paul Jackson. Through this teaching, I received many revelations and mysteries regarding the Bible. For example, Sir Isaac Newton was an English mathematician, physicist, astronomer, theologian, and author. He was recognised as one of the most influential scientists of all time. A key figure in the scientific revolution who discovered light shining through a prism produced a rainbow effect.

A prism is a glass or other transparent object, especially one that is triangular with refracting surfaces at an acute angle with each other. It separates white light into a spectrum of seven colours: red, orange, yellow, green, blue, indigo, and violet. A triangular prism has three sides and two bases. The two bases of this prism are equilateral triangles, and the edges of these triangles are parallel. The prism's symbolic meaning with the three sides represents the Trinity *(Father, Son, Holy Spirit)*.

The prophet Ezekiel received an open vision of heaven and God, and recorded it as follows, *"Like the appearance of a rainbow in the clouds on a rainy day, so was the radiance around Him. This was the appearance of the likeness of the glory of the Lord. When I saw it, I fell facedown, and I heard the voice of one speaking."* (Ezekiel 1:28).

The number '7' is also significant to God. So, the light he consists of through a prism gives seven colours, which forms a rainbow. Earth was created in seven days. There will come a seven-year tribulation at the end of this age. In the revelation that Jesus gave the apostle John about the end times, he saw the following in an open vision: The Lord *(Jesus)* has the seven Spirits of God and the seven stars (Revelation 3:1). Seven lamps of fire are burning before God's throne in heaven, which are the seven Spirits of God (Revelation 4:5). In the midst of the throne and the four living creatures, and the elders, stood a Lamb *(Jesus)* as though it had been slain, having seven horns and seven eyes, which are the seven Spirits of God sent out into all the earth (Revelation 5:6). The Book of Revelation also mentions the seven churches, seven angels, seven seals, seven trumpets. When Peter asked Jesus how many times we are to forgive each other, Jesus replied, 'seventy times seven times' (Matthew 18:21-22). The prophet Elisha referenced the number seven when he directed Naaman the leper to bathe in the Jordan River seven times to be healed (2 Kings 5:9-10,14). In Genesis, after Noah's flood, God promised never to destroy the earth again with water and gave us the rainbow as a sign of the covenant, comprising of seven colours (Genesis 9:8-15). God promised Joshua that He'd bring down Jericho's fortified walls if Joshua and his army would march around the city once for six days and seven times on the seventh day, with seven priests blowing seven trumpets (Joshua 6:1-20). There are many more examples in the Bible where seven signifies something important.

Let's now look at an explanation of how everything on earth was created. A scientist will have more in-depth teaching on this! All things, even humans and animals, are made of atoms. Science reveals that an atom is composed of a nucleus and electrons. Even smaller particles *(protons and neutrons)* make up the nucleus. Particle physics has further discovered that protons and neutrons are a collection of microscopic light particles called 'quarks'. *Quarks* have a constant interchange of even smaller substances called 'gluons' and 'mesons' comprised of colour and anti-colours incessantly moving in and out of the quark. Therefore, all of creation is made up of these quarks. The important thing is that these subatomic particles are nothing more than pure white light. In other words, the entirety of creation is made of light, and God is light! And God created mankind in His image (Genesis 1:26-27, Genesis 9:6).

Thinking of God's first recorded words in the Bible, 'Let there be light' (Genesis 1:3). This pronouncement created the substance from which all things were made, and that substance is light. Paul said in Romans 1:20, *"For since the creation of the world His invisible attributes are clearly seen, being understood by the things that are made, even His eternal power and Godhead, so that they are without excuse."*

There are three colour spectrums: additive spectrum, subtractive spectrum, and the artist's spectrum, representing the three different components of the human body. Each of the colour spectrums has three primary and three secondary colours.

The Additive Spectrum (Spirit):

This spectrum deals with light, not pigments. It radiates colour rather than reflecting or absorbing it.

i. Primary colours: red, blue, green.

ii. Secondary colours: yellow, cyan, magenta.

Combining these six colours of light result in white or transparent light. Therefore, this is the spectrum of the Spirit.

The Subtractive Spectrum (Soul):

When light illuminates an object, the colours that are seen are those that are reflected back to the eye. The item you see absorbs all other colours. Thus, colours are subtracted from those that are seen.

i. Primary colours: yellow, cyan, magenta.

ii. Secondary colours: red, blue, green.

This spectrum *reflects* colour. All the colours combined construct an opaque black colour in the centre or middle. This spectrum represents the soul.

The Artist Spectrum (Body):

The object absorbs the colour that we see.

i. Primary colours: yellow, red, blue.

ii. Secondary colours: orange, green, violet

This spectrum *absorbs* colour. In other words, some colours become distinct as the object absorbs different colours from the light that shines on it. These colours combined produce a colour which is near black or very dark brown. When we study colour in the Bible, we find some fascinating parallels with this colour spectrums' colour.

SPIRIT: The three colours of the Spirit are: red, blue, and green. The three aspects of the spirit are wisdom, communion (or revelation), and conscience.

SOUL: The three colours of the soul are: yellow, magenta, and cyan. The three aspects of the soul are mind, emotions, and will.

FLESH: The three colours of the body are: yellow, red, and blue. The three aspects of the body are flesh, blood, and bone.

Jesus made an interesting statement about light and darkness within a person. He said in Matthew 6:23, *"If your eye is bad, your whole body will be full of darkness. If therefore the light that is in you is darkness, great is that darkness."* In making parallels with quantum physics, we can say that Jesus acknowledged the existence of 'dark light'. He stated that this dark light could fill our whole being. When our soul rules us *(mind, will, and emotions)*, the light of God shines less brightly within us.

Consequently, we lack spiritual perception, and we live in spiritual darkness. Light and colour are, therefore, significant to God. Many people who visited heaven in physical form, or a dream, testified that heaven's colours look more radiant and alive than those on earth. The reason may be because God's perfect light illuminates everything, and there is no darkness found in heaven. Some also said there are many more beautiful colours in heaven that we do not see on earth.

How we are created in God's image are as follows:

- God is light, and our bodies are tiny particles of light.

- God has free will, and He also gave us free will.

- God has emotions of anger, hurt, etc. We experience the same feelings.

- God created us as His children and loves us very much, and He wants us to love Him too. Just as we want to have children we can love, we would like them to love us.

- God is creative because He created the heavens, and the earth, and everything in it. His people are also creative in painting, drawing, building beautiful buildings and gardens, designing beautiful interior decorated houses, etc.

- God has authority over the devil, the fallen angels, and everything evil. God also gave His people authority over the devil and his demons through Jesus Christ.

- God created everything through speaking. Jesus taught us that life and death are in the power of the tongue. In other words, through speaking positively, we can create a promising future for ourselves. Even our bodies can heal by saying and believing it.

CHAPTER 4

SPIRITUAL WARFARE

Why is spiritual warfare necessary? Ephesians 6:12 says that our struggles are not against flesh and blood *(people)*, but against the rulers, against the authorities, against the powers of this dark world and the spiritual forces of evil in the heavenly realms *(evil spirits)*. It is not whether you want to be in this war or not, because everyone is in it! Either we are defeated by the devil, or we resist him.

Through years of experience and listening to different preachers, evangelists, and missionaries, I have tested many things regarding spiritual warfare. The Bible teaches us how to win battles against the devil and his demons.

The most successful weapon to overcome spiritual forces coming against us is the Word of God. In Hebrews 4:12-13, we read the following, *"For the Word of God is living and active, sharper than any two-edged sword, piercing to the division of soul and of spirit, of joints and of marrow, and discerning the thoughts and intentions of the heart. And no creature is hidden from His sight, but all are naked and exposed to the eyes of Him to whom we must give account."*

Revelation 2:12 says, *"And to the angel of the church in Pergamos write, 'These things says He (Jesus) who has the sharp two-edged sword....'"* In Ephesians 6:17, Paul refers to the Word of God as the helmet of salvation and the sword of the Spirit. Apart from knowing that a two-edged sword is very sharp in real life, I always wondered why God refers to His Word as a two-edged sword. That is until I heard a Bible teacher explain what God had shown him. His explanation sounded so right that it stuck with me! He said that when God spoke His words in the Bible, He put a blade on the sword, and when we speak the exact words, we put another blade on the sword. So the Word *(Bible)* coming out of God's mouth, then the Word *(Bible)* coming out of our mouth forms a two-edged sword, which becomes the weapon of our warfare!

That is how easy it is to overcome the devil and his evil spirits by speaking the Word of God! The problem is that many people do not regularly study the Word of God to build their knowledge and be able to recall the scriptures when they are fighting spiritual battles. During Jesus' first coming to earth, after He got baptised by John the Baptist, He was led into the wilderness by the Holy Spirit to be tempted by the devil for forty days and forty nights. During the entire time of this spiritual battle, He was fasting. While He was tempted at other times throughout His life on earth, this period in the wilderness severely tested how He would respond to temptation. It serves as an example to us and demonstrates His ability to wrestle with temptation and overcome it. After fasting for forty days, He was clearly hungry, but when Satan came to Him and tempted Him by saying, *"If you are the Son of God, tell these stones to become bread."* Jesus quoted Deuteronomy 8:3 to him, *'**It is written**, Man shall not live by bread alone, but by every word that proceedeth out of the mouth of God."* (Matthew 4:4). This is how Jesus used Scripture as a two-edged sword!

Then Satan took Jesus to Jerusalem and had Him stand on the highest point of the temple. Satan quoted the Old Testament by saying to Him, *"If you are the Son of God, throw yourself down. For it is written: He will command His angels concerning you, and they will lift you up in their hands, so that You will not strike your foot against a stone."* Jesus answered him again by quoting scripture from Deuteronomy 6:6, *'**It is also written**: Do not put the Lord your God to the test."* (Matthew 4:5-7).

Again, Satan took Jesus to a very high mountain and showed Him all the kingdoms of the world and their splendour, and he said to Jesus, *"All this I will give you, if you will bow down and worship me."* Jesus then quoted a third time to Satan from Deuteronomy 6:13-15, *"Away from me, Satan!* **For it is written**: *Worship the Lord your God, and serve Him only."* Then the devil left him, and angels came and attended Him (Matthew 4:10-11).

If the devil tempted Jesus, who is God, he would come for us in the same way. Satan knows the Bible very well! That is why we have to know it very well to use it against him as a two-edged sword. When we resist Satan by quoting Scripture, he will flee from us! At the beginning of the Bible, it shows us how powerful it is when God speaks. Earth and everything in it was created through God's spoken Word and the power of the Holy Spirit. In other words, God spoke everything into existence, and His Power *(The Holy Spirit)* created it (Genesis 1:1-31, Psalm 33:6, Psalm 33:9).

Revelation 19:11-21 describes the return of Jesus Christ to earth. In verse 15, we read, *"Now out of His mouth goes a sharp sword, that with it He should strike the nations."* This sharp sword refers to the Word *(Bible)*, which is also a reference to Jesus Christ. The Bible teach us that Jesus is the Word. In John 1:1, we read, *"In the beginning was the Word, and the Word was with God, and the Word was God."* And John 1:14 says, *"And the Word became flesh and dwelt among us, and we have seen His glory, glory as of the only Son from the Father, full of grace and truth."* He (Jesus) was with God in the beginning. Through Him, all things were made; without Him, nothing was made that has been made. In Him was life, and that life was the light of all mankind. The light shines in the darkness, and the darkness has not overcome it."

The Battle Between the Two Kingdoms

A good God created a good universe and earth, but it was corrupted when evil entered in. God was not content to leave His good creation to the corruption of sin and is still working to defeat evil and restore His creation. Genesis 3:15 marked the beginning of spiritual warfare between humanity and Satan when God prophesied, *"I will put enmity between you and the woman, and between your seed and her Seed; He shall bruise your head, and you shall bruise His heel."* The **Seed** of the woman *(Mary)* refers to **Jesus Christ**, who would have come in the future and be born of a virgin when God said it. 'The seed of the woman' points to a virgin birth because, typically, birth comes from the seed of a man.

The battle of God versus Satan has been going on for over 6,000 years, and spiritual warfare will continue until Jesus finally defeats the devil at the end of this current age. God has not left this world under the complete control of Satan, but the fullness of God's Kingdom will not come about until this present evil age comes to an end. God has not been dethroned. The destruction of Satan's stronghold has already been guaranteed through Christ's death, burial, and resurrection from the dead. The cross, therefore, restricted Satan's power up to now. Revelation 12:11 says this about faithful Christians, *"They overcame him (Satan) by the blood of the Lamb (Jesus), and by the word of their testimony."* The Satanic realm functions on multiple fronts that make up our societies: cultural, economic, political, and religious. The Bible makes it clear that Satan's evil influence over mankind is destined to end. I surely cannot wait for that time!

In Daniel 10, the prophet Daniel received a troubling vision concerning a great war coming. He went into three weeks of mourning, fasting, and prayer. In response to Daniel's prayer, God sent a messenger from heaven to explain the vision. However, the messenger was delayed for twenty-one days because the prince of the Kingdom of Persia *(evil spirit)* resisted him. Then Michael, one of God's chief princes, came to help him. Just before the messenger left Daniel, he said in verses 20-21, *"Soon I will return to fight against the prince of Persia, and when I go, the prince of Greece will come, but first I will tell you what is written in the Book of Truth (Bible)."* This is how the devil and evil spirits can hinder God's responses to our prayers! We cannot deny their existence because the Bible teaches us of their works. Thank God that we can resist them through the finished work of Jesus on the cross and knowledge of God's Word.

The Kingdom of God is not yet a reality on earth. Jesus instructed the members of His Church to preach the Gospel to all nations. At the final judgment, the nations will be divided into sheep and goat nations, i.e. those that have blessed His brethren, the Jews (sheep nations) and those who have not (goat nations) - Matthew 25:31-46.

Jesus included many parables that explain the Kingdom of Heaven and that it has not yet replaced the kingdoms of this world, but the seeds of the future government of Christ have been planted and are growing. There is a time coming when the kingdom of this world will become the kingdom of our Lord Jesus, and He will reign over the earth forever (Revelation 11:15).

Ten Things Satan Wants for Your Life

1. ***To doubt God*** - In John 20, the disciples said that they had seen Jesus raised from the dead, but for one disciple, Thomas, doubt kept him from believing in the miracle of the resurrection. Jesus appeared to Thomas and said, "Stop doubting and believe" (John 20:27).

2. ***To avoid the church or not to believe in Almighty God*** *(God the Father, Jesus, Holy Spirit)* - The more uninvolved one becomes with the body of Christ, the harder it is to persevere in faith. If a person does not believe in Almighty God, Satan is not worried because he's got them right where he wants them. One of his main focuses is to pull a believer away from other believers to be more vulnerable to target on their own.

3. ***To live in fear*** - Fear is not the absence of faith; it is the misplacement of it. The devil doesn't want to rob us of our faith; he wants our faith to be in anything but God. 1 Peter 5:6-7 says, *"Humble yourselves, therefore, under God's mighty hand, that He may lift you up in due time. Cast all your anxiety on Him because He cares for you."* Jesus said in John 14:27, *"Peace I leave with you; my peace I give you. I do not give to you as the world gives. Do not let your hearts be troubled, and do not be afraid."*

4. ***To feel insecure*** – If a person does not have confidence in who they are and who God created them to be, they fall prey to Satan's lies. He loves breaking down God's creation. He hates everything and everyone who worships God. Those who do not understand who they are in Christ easily believe Satan's lies about who they are. My book *Clothed for the King* explains in detail how to gain confidence in who we are in Christ.

5. ***To be led astray*** – Satan wants followers of Christ to go in the wrong direction, away from God. The best way to do that is to mislead them from the truth. In Matthew 7:15, we read, *"Beware of false prophets, who come to you in sheep's clothing but inwardly are ravenous wolves."* Many people belong to a church or organisation that uses the Bible as their foundation, but changes are made to the truth. Some Christian churches do it unknowingly because they interpret the Bible differently. Other churches and organisations do it deliberately to mislead people. This is when Satan works through the leaders to lead God's people astray. Many do not realise it because they do not study the Bible themselves or did not become a born again believer so that the Holy Spirit can teach them.

God warns us not to take any of His words out of the Bible or add words to it. In Deuteronomy 4:2, He said, *"Do not add to what I command you and do not subtract from it, but keep the commands of the Lord your God that I give you."* In Deuteronomy 12:32, God also said, *"See that you do all I command you; do not add to it or take away from it."* And *in Revelation 22:18-19,* Jesus said, *"I warn everyone who hears the words of the prophecy of this scroll: If anyone adds anything to them, God will add to that person the plagues described in this scroll. And if anyone takes words away from this scroll of prophecy, God will take away from that person any share in the tree of life and in the Holy City, which are described in this scroll."*

There are many religions and organisations that are guilty of this sin. I'll discuss only two examples. Let's look at *Islam* and *Mormonism*. Islam does not acknowledge Jesus Christ as the Son of God and the Messiah who came to save the world from sin. They recognise Jesus as a prophet and miracle worker. According to Islam, Satan is responsible for sin, and there is no curse over Adam or creation. Islam believes that Jesus was born of a virgin and that He ascended into Heaven, but they do not believe that He died on the cross. The God of Islam is one God, therefore one person, not a Trinity as described in the Holy Bible. Muslims believe their *Quran* was revealed to the prophet Muhammad from the angel Gabriel over twenty-three years, beginning in 609 A.D. *(anno domini)*.

In contrast, the Bible contains sixty-six books, written by forty authors inspired by the Holy Spirit, and took approximately one thousand five hundred years to complete. Throughout history, they proved to be true witnesses of God. The first book was written by Moses around 1400 B.C. *(before Christ)*, and the apostle John wrote the last book around 90 A.D. They speculate that the book of Job is the oldest in the Bible, and some have suggested that Moses wrote it. The author's name is not indicated, but Job was a real person according to Ezekiel 14:14-20 and James 5:11.

Muslims recognize the Torah *(law)* of Moses, Psalms of David, and the Gospels of Jesus as books from God. However, they believe these writings have been corrupted over time due to the many different translations. Muslims claim that no manuscript of the Quran in Arabic has any variation and is perfect. Christians believe that the Old and New Testaments in their original languages *(Hebrew, Greek, Aramaic)* are God's Word without error. Our English Bibles today are still trustworthy because of textual criticism.

The church of Mormonism is called *The Church of Jesus Christ of Latter-Day Saints (LDS)*. Their holy book is called the *Book of Mormon*, which was first published in 1830 in Palmyra, New York. The Book of Mormon resembles the Bible in its length and complexity and its division into books named for individual prophets. It relates the history of a group of Hebrews who migrated from Jerusalem to America about 600 B.C., led by a prophet, Lehi. They multiplied and eventually split into two groups. One group, the Lamanites, who forgot their beliefs, became heathens and were the ancestors of the American Indians. The other group, the Nephites, developed culturally and built great cities but were eventually destroyed by the Lamanites about 400 A.D. However, before that occurred, they believe Jesus appeared after His ascension and taught the Nephites. According to the book itself, the history and teachings of Jesus were abridged and written on gold plates by the prophet Mormon. His son, Moroni, made additions and buried the plates in the ground, where they remained for about 1,400 years until Moroni appeared as a resurrected being or angel and delivered them to Joseph Smith. They say Moroni instructed him to translate the characters engraved on their surfaces with the aid of unique stones called 'interpreters.' Smith insisted that he did not compose the book but merely 'translated' it under divine guidance. He completed the work in less than 90 days.

The Mormons believe that God is a created being. We, like God the Father, all have the opportunity to ascend just like He did, 'As God now is, man will one day be...'. So, while a Mormon will affirm there is 'One God', they do not mean it as Christians do. They believe there is one God of planet earth. Elsewhere there are other gods. There are gods all over the place! All someday to be worthy of worship and adoration. To Mormons, Jesus is one of God's many sons and is just a man, not God Himself. They are not sure of salvation through the cross and do not believe it is free. They think they have to earn it.

6. ***To miss out on the full blessings from God*** - God has promised to abundantly bless those who submit their lives to Him in obedience. Job 36:11 tells us that those who obey and serve God will spend their days in prosperity and their years in pleasures. Psalm 1:3 says, whatever the righteous do,

he will prosper. Satan is working very hard to get people to fall away from God and not receive His blessings.

7. ***To go to hell at the end of this age*** - Jesus talked more about Hell than He did about Heaven. Why? Because He wanted people to understand that Hell is not a place anyone should want to go. It is a place of extreme darkness! It's separated from God and light. Satan's most effective plan is to get as many of God's people as possible to go to hell with him. Why? Because he wants to destroy all of God's good creation. Those who reject Christ choose to follow Satan, and they will follow him right into his ultimate destination, despite all that God has done to save them from the fiery abyss. Hell is forever! All who enter hell, abandon all hope!

8. ***To suffer while on earth*** - Matthew 4:3 calls Satan 'the tempter'. He wants to tempt us, so we go the wrong way and suffer because of our bad decisions. Suffering may include physical pain, psychological pain, heartache, and financial hardships. Job's story is an example of how Satan wants to harm people, especially those who believe in God and are followers of Christ. He delights in scarring people so that he can go back and attack them later. Our sinful choices often leave deep scars in our life and the lives of our children. Satan will not miss an opportunity to rip the wounds open later in life. In Luke 16:22-24, we read of a rich man and a poor man. First, the poor man *(Lazarus)* died, and the angels carried him to Abraham's side, in other words, on the side where Abraham was. It was the side where all the God-fearing people were kept until Jesus made atonement for their sins on the cross. After Lazarus died, the rich man died and was tormented in Hades *(In Greek mythology, Hades is both the land of the dead and the god who rules there)*. It was thought to be a place under or in the middle of the earth, where wicked people are temporarily punished (Matthew 11:23). The rich man saw in the distance Father Abraham and Lazarus at his side. And he called out, *"Father Abraham, have mercy on me, and send Lazarus to dip the end of his finger in*

water and cool my tongue, for I am in anguish in this flame." (Luke 16:24).

I've heard of testimonies similar to the above scripture where people died and went to hell or were taken in a vision to see hell so they could come and testify to us of their experience. All spoke of the same things; that is the torment they had seen or experienced. The evil spirits in hell took great pleasure in tormenting people. That is one of Satan's desires, to see people suffer on earth and later in hell. When Jesus Christ died on the cross, He descended into hell. Acts 2:31 says He was not abandoned to hell, nor did His body see corruption. Matthew 12:40 reads, *"For as Jonas was three days and three nights in the whale's belly: so shall the Son of man be three days and three nights in the HEART OF THE EARTH."* Why did Jesus descend into hell? It was as a triumphant king proclaiming His victory over sin, death, and the devil, and announcing it to all the saints who died before Him, like Abraham, Sarah, David, Noah, and many others, bringing them to heaven (Ephesians 4:9, Acts 2:24, 1 Peter 3:19, Hosea 13:14, Zechariah 9:11, Colossians 2:15).

9. *To break up family relations* - The ways Satan and his demons work to break up families are endless! He might induce a husband or wife to put too much emphasis on their career or to spend a lot of time pursuing material wealth, a beautiful house, and a car. He may tempt them by sending another person so that they are unfaithful to their spouse. If these strategies do not work, he may use greed, lust, pornography, drug and alcohol addiction to drive a wedge between them. Their children may even be stirred up with rebellion to break up a family. Why does the devil desire to break up the family? Because he is breaking up the unity of love and protection. That makes each member vulnerable on their own, and the psychological loss will make them want to find love and acceptance in unconventional ways or with the wrong crowd. Through issues in the family unit, Satan keeps the members so busy that they do not have time

to know God. Satan aims to get family members to put the love of themselves and their pleasures ahead of loving God.

God has a plan for our lives, but Satan also has a plan, which is not good. He wants to get our minds off God and keep us busy. In John 10:10, Jesus said, *"The thief (Satan) does not come except to steal, and to kill, and to destroy. I (Jesus) have come that they may have life and that they may have it more abundantly."*

10. ***To kill humankind as soon as possible, and where possible in the womb*** - Satan wants to kill people quickly so that they do not have the time to get right with their Heavenly Father. The push to legalise abortion in all countries is just one strategy of his. Another way he works is by possessing people to follow a religion where they have to offer babies and people to him during their rituals.

How To Resist Satan

James said, *"Resist the devil, and he will flee from you!"* (James 4:7) Resist by being firm in your faith.

- Repent of your sins and accept Jesus Christ as your Lord and Saviour, then continue to repent daily for known and unknown sins that you may have committed.

- The blood of the Lamb defeated Satan. Jesus conquered Satan on the cross (Revelation 12:11). Therefore we are conquerors through Jesus Christ by believing it, speaking it, and taking communion often to celebrate it.

- Read the Word of God daily. We had already seen how Jesus quoted Scripture when Satan tempted Him in the wilderness in a previous chapter. The Word of God is the power that overcomes the devil. Paul said in Ephesians 6:16, *"In all circumstances, take up the shield of faith, with which you can extinguish all the flaming darts of the evil one."* What is faith? *"Faith comes by hearing, and hearing by the Word of God."* - Romans 10:17.

- Pray and worship regularly. Morning and night, or at any time when you get a prompting from the Holy Spirit. Play worship music during the day. Apostle Paul said in 1 Thessalonians 5:16-18, *"Rejoice always, pray without ceasing, give thanks in all circumstances; for this is the will of God in Christ Jesus for you."* Pray often for your family and friends. Even Jesus fought against the devil on our behalf with the weapon of prayer. He said to Peter in Luke 22:31-32, *"Satan has asked to have you that he might sift you like wheat, but I have prayed for you that your faith may not fail."*

In Matthew 6:7-8, Jesus said to His disciples, *"When you pray, do not heap up empty phrases as the Gentiles do, for they think that they will be heard for their many words. Do not be like them, for your Father knows what you need before you ask Him."* Jesus then said, pray like this:

The Lord's Prayer

Our Father in heaven,
Hallowed be your name,
Your kingdom come,
Your will be done,
On earth, as it is in heaven.
Give us today our daily bread.
And forgive us our debts,
As we also have forgiven our debtors.
And lead us not into temptation,
But deliver us from the evil one.
(Matthew 6:9-13)

The Lord's Prayer covers all bases, and it is good to pray every morning before your day starts. Print it or write it out, and stick it on a prominent spot that will remind you to pray after you woke up and see how it transforms your life.

Binding Evil Spirits That May Be Interfering in Your Life

The most crucial strategy against Satan and his demons is the acknowledgement of their existence. Not believing that they exist places us in a very vulnerable position. However, focusing on this realm too much is spiritually unhealthy. The essential thing is to know your Bible, focus on your relationship with God, and learn to see the difference between the urging of Satan and the gentle nudge of the Holy Spirit. Ephesians 6:10-17 teaches us to put on the 'full armour of God' and how to defend ourselves against the devil's schemes.

Apart from the Word of God, I have found that an essential weapon in binding a demon or evil spirit who is trying to destroy us is discernment, which is a gift of the Holy Spirit. We must first identify the demon before we can successfully bind it. Then we also have to recognise when they want to come back into our life.

Demons have a lot of patience and will wait for an open door in our life to enter again. In Matthew 12:43-45, Jesus taught His disciples the following: *"When an impure spirit comes out of a person, it goes through arid places seeking rest and does not find it. Then it says, 'I will return to the house I left.' When it arrives, it finds the house unoccupied, swept clean, and put in order. Then it goes and takes with it seven other spirits more wicked than itself, and they go in and live there. And the final condition of that person is worse than the first."*

After deciding to get rid of an addiction or unrighteous trait, how can a person protect themselves from the same unclean spirits trying to tempt them again? By staying away from the same temptation, filling one's mind with the knowledge of God, and being guided by the Holy Spirit. The apostle Peter taught about being vigilant in 1 Peter 5:8-9, *"Be alert and of sober mind. Your enemy, the devil, prowls around like a roaring lion looking for someone to devour. Resist him, standing firm in the faith, because you know that the family of believers throughout the world is undergoing the same kind of sufferings."*

In Corinthians 12, the apostle Paul discusses the Holy Spirit's gifts, and in verse 10, he mentions that 'discerning of spirits' is one.

Discerning means to recognise whether or not something is truly from God and compares well with righteousness. Being sensitive to the Holy Spirit will allow us to discern between His voice and the enemy's voice, between God's works and the enemy's works.

One common rule is that if we do not call a person by their name, they will not listen or act. The spirit world works the same way! If we do not address the specific demon or evil spirit by name, they do not listen. Let's take the example of when a person has an alcohol addiction. We will not have success in binding the spirit of jealousy but need to call it by name. I have heard testimonies about some people who went through deliverance that the controlling evil spirit resisted leaving and often revealed their identity or name as the alcohol brand they were addicted to, like Jack Daniels, Johnny Walker, or Vodka.

Another vital thing to know is that there are always strong men in Satan's spiritual hierarchy, which have many sub-demons under them. Remember that Satan was one of the chief angels in heaven. He was a Guardian Cherub, the seal of perfection, blameless in all his ways until wickedness was found in him. He was in charge of a large section of angels, and as such, he had a divinely given organisational system. When he rebelled against God and led the angels under him in rebellion, he simply took the system God invented and turned it against God. This organisational system consists of Satan at the top, followed by rulers, followed by sub-rules with various areas of authority, and most likely under them will be sub-sub rulers with smaller areas of authority. Never think that Satan does not have a highly organised kingdom. He is a powerful and evil being! Therefore, binding a sub-demon may not be successful, as we have to bind the strongman or head ruler to get rid of all the sub and sub-sub rulers too!

When a person struggles with demonic oppression or possession, we have to pray for the Holy Spirit's guidance. There is no clear explanation of how the Satanic hierarchy fits together, but we know bits and pieces from our Bible study. The Word of God promises us that the Holy Spirit will reveal mysterious things to us. God said to the prophet Jeremiah, *"Call to Me, and I will answer you, and show you great and mighty things, which you do not know."* (Jeremiah 33:3). From experience, I know that if I ask God to reveal the unseen to me, He does it at the right time and when it is going to make a difference.

Let's look again at the example of a person with an addiction. Have you noticed that many people with an addiction are usually addicted to more than one substance? An alcoholic is typically a smoker and may have other addictions like smoking marijuana or using methamphetamine. Often they are also addicted to painkillers or prescription medications. Other characteristics may be arrogance, sexual sins, trying to be religious, being undisciplined, having suicidal thoughts, being unforgiving, having feelings of insecurity, is unreasonable, critical, rebellious, and has a fear of rejection.

By looking at all the above characteristics of an addict, I'll place the hierarchical structure something like this:

- *At the top:* Satan is the god of all evil.

- *As the ruler:* Jezebel.

- *Sub-rulers:*
  1) Addiction.
  2) Rebellion.
  3) Unforgiveness.
  4) Pride.

- *Sub-sub-rulers:*
  1) Alcohol, cigarettes, marijuana, painkillers, methamphetamine.
  2) Sexual sins, undisciplined, unreasonable.
  3) Fear, suicidal thoughts, insecurity, rejection.
  4) Religious, criticizing, arrogance.

I'll explain more about discernment in the following sections, which will put it all into context.

The Three Realms

There are three realms of discernment that we must be aware of to identify the spirit we are dealing with:

1. ***The Spirit of God*** - The Holy Spirit is the Spirit of God and the Spirit of Christ (Job 33:4, Romans 8:9). The first thing to understand is that to recognise the Holy Spirit, we need to have a relationship with God. It begins when we recognise our need for Him, admitting that we fall short as sinners, and by faith receiving Jesus Christ as our Lord and Saviour. As soon as we've done this, we receive the Holy Spirit, who will begin to work in our hearts. We must include God then in our daily life by reading, studying, and meditating on the Bible; praying; talking to God; and waiting for Him to speak to us. 1 Corinthians 2:14 says, *"The person without the Spirit does not accept the things that come from the Spirit of God but considers them foolishness, and cannot understand them because they are discerned only through the Spirit."*

The Holy Spirit works as follows:

- He will never contradict the Bible. He testifies to us who God is, who Christ is, and what God's Word means.

- He is known as the Comforter and calms our fears, filling our hearts with hope.

- He bears witness to the truth and is also called the Spirit of Truth (John 16:13).

- The Spirit is not tied to things of the flesh. He focuses on Spiritual things (Romans 8:9).

- His voice is unique, and He does not talk to us as the world does. His voice is gentle and persuasive, free from pressure and domination. You'll hear Him in your heart when your mind races or when other voices are distracting you.

- Jesus referred to the Holy Spirit as our teacher in John 14:26, who will teach us everything that God and Jesus teach us in the Bible.

- Listen for messages that are repeated by different unrelated sources. The Holy Spirit usually works through confirmation.

- He also communicates with us through visions and dreams.

- He often speaks to us very early in the morning, when the world is still asleep and everything is quiet. Generally, between 2-6 am, before sunrise.

- The Holy Spirit will convict us when we are wrong. No amount of preaching or pointing of fingers will bring about the conviction of sin unless the Holy Spirit is at work in the sinner's heart. He is not unkind but a loving teacher.

- Signs and wonders follow the Holy Spirit. His creating power hovered over the waters when God and Jesus created the earth and everything in it (Genesis 1:1-2). He raised Jesus from the dead (Romans 8:11). When the power of the Holy Spirit came over the disciples, they performed the same miracles as Jesus Christ did (Read the whole of Acts 2).

- The Holy Spirit gives us courage and confidence.

- He also gives us the peace of God, which surpasses all understanding (Philippians 4:7).

- His voice is always clear and distinctive, giving us clear direction. We just have to learn to recognise His voice.

- The Holy Spirit is always encouraging and uplifting. Never condemning (Romans 8:1).

2. ***The Spirit of the Enemy*** - The Bible refers to our enemies as the following: Satan, devil/s, demons, unclean spirits, and evil spirits. There is a name above all names in the world, which is Jesus Christ, and Satan's evil spirits cannot

say this name. 'Jesus' alone without 'Christ' does not rattle them, but 'Jesus Christ' acknowledges that Jesus is the Christ. In the name of Jesus Christ, apostles and anointed men of God performed miracles and signs. Christ means: The Messiah, Anointed One, or Chosen One. Jesus is His name, and Christ is His title. He is the Saviour sent from God and redeemed us from the curse of the law (Galatians 3:10-13). I've heard a story told by Evangelist Robert Breaker when he asked an ex-devil worshipper about the evil realm. Some demons also bear the name Jesus. Therefore we have to carefully test a person or a spirit who may appear to us. In 2 Corinthians 11:14-15, we read, *"And no wonder! For Satan, himself transforms himself into an angel of light. Therefore it is no great thing if his ministers also transform themselves into ministers of righteousness, whose end will be according to their works."*

With darkness rising in this world, we need the gift of discerning spirits since not all supernatural activity comes from the Holy Spirit.

The evil spirits from the enemy work as follows:

- Through stirring up fear in us.

- They come to kill, steal and destroy.

- They want to control, manipulate, dominate and distract.

- They come to us via thoughts of pride, hate, jealousy, revenge, killing, stealing, worthlessness, rebellion, unforgiveness, unhappiness, failure, and negative thoughts.

- Satan's voice is loud and clamouring, always demanding an immediate response. In an uncomfortable or heated situation, we always want to respond straight away, but we must think things through first and ask the Holy Spirit's guidance before we react.

- The voice of the enemy is usually confusing with loss of direction.

- When the enemy is behind something, we lose all hope and are feeling overwhelmed.

- The enemy always oppresses people and is the master of lies.

- Using slander to steal, kill and destroy! Be careful what you say! Loose lips are the greatest weapon that the enemy has in the world. Many times we are causing our own warfare with what we speak. Do not let the enemy have access to your tongue! (Proverbs 18:21 and Proverbs 13:3).

- He wants to keep us busy with gossip. Avoid gossip, as we will account for every idle word (Matthew 12:36 and Romans 14:12).

3. *The Spirit of Oneself* - This is our spirit, which is the third part of the human body. In 1 Thessalonians 5:23, the apostle Paul wrote, *"May God himself, the God of peace, sanctify you through and through. May your whole spirit, soul, and body be kept blameless at the coming of our Lord Jesus Christ."* In John 4:24, we read, *"God is a Spirit: and they that worship Him must worship Him in spirit and in truth."* This means our spirit must connect with God through the Holy Spirit, so we can hear Him better. Worshipping in the Spirit is to look past the flesh or the things we can see and look through the eyes of faith.

    Proverbs 16:32 says, *"He who is slow to anger is better than the mighty, and he who rules his spirit than he who takes a city."* Therefore, when we control our emotions like anger, fear, disgust, surprise, joy, interest, and sadness, our spirit is overcoming our fleshly desires. Being out of control is what the Bible describes as 'the works of the flesh'. The flesh doesn't just refer to our physical body, but the old nature or characteristics we inherited from our parents. We can't blame them because they inherited it from their parents, and their parents inherited it from theirs, all the way back to Adam and Eve.

    Our spirit will usually think more in fleshly terms, and we have to be conscious of that fact. We must teach our spirit to control our fleshly desires and connect with the Holy Spirit. In Philippians 3:3, the apostle Paul says this to the children of God: *"For it is we who are the circumcision, we who serve God by his Spirit, who boast in Christ Jesus, and who put no confidence in the flesh."*

How do we know if the desires in our heart are ours or God's? Before we begin pursuing our heart's desires, we must test if they line up with God's Word and will. Following are three key points:

1. *A door that God opens will never contradict His Word.* For example, God will not give His children a career that harms themselves or others, like opening a liquor store, selling drugs, going into a partnership where a business has to run illegal or inhumane operations to make money, etc.

2. Usually, a *door that God opens is accompanied by confirmation.* For example, A man or woman of God gives a prophecy regarding one's life or situation. A confirmation often comes twice but can be more, and many times comes from a godly person we do not know well. Other confirmations are through the soft, indwelling voice of the Holy Spirit or when we are reading or hearing the Word of God. We can even receive confirmation of something through a dream.

3. *A door that God opens will require a person to depend on Him.* For example, He'll not give you millions of dollars but will provide you with a job to provide enough to live day-by-day to stay humble and pray regularly for His provision. God wants us to serve and trust Him daily. The biggest problem in many peoples' lives is that they live above their means. That is why some lose faith, thinking that God does not look after them well enough, whereas the problem is, they put themselves under the stress of barely making it.

Discerning Strongholds in Your Life

Usually, when we are in the centre of God's plan, we have the most satanic opposition. Everybody is prone to strongholds, and it does not matter if they are a believer or unbeliever. The level of the stronghold/s in our life is dependent on how much authority we give to the devil. The good news is, the stronger we build our knowledge of the Bible and live out our faith in God, the harder it will be for Satan and his demons to have a hold over us.

How does the devil get a stronghold over us? It usually starts small. Then it grows bigger if we do not recognize him to stop it in time. An example is when a person has worked hard during the day, and they just want to relax with a glass of wine in the evening. After a while, a glass of wine may become two glasses of wine in the evening. Followed by half a bottle, then ending in a bottle of wine a night. Another open door is if we believe his constant lies and accusations. In Revelation 12:10, the apostle John heard a loud voice in heaven saying, *"Now the salvation and the power and the kingdom of our God and the authority of his Christ have come, for the accuser of our brothers has been thrown down, who accuses them day and night before our God."* Satan is the accuser! Has always been, and will always be!

How is it possible for a person to have a demon or demons in them or around them? The answer is that a person or someone else has given them authority. It can happen consciously or unconsciously. Satan and his demons have so many tricks to get a stronghold in a person's life, and when it happens unconsciously, it is harder to discern. Here are a few examples to be aware of as a child of God that can give an open door:

- Hurts or disappointments make our hearts fertile ground for seeds of lies to be planted.

- Unconfessed sins in our life where we think God will never forgive us. The Biblical fact is that there is no sin in our life that is so great which the blood of Jesus hasn't already paid. However, what we keep hidden will remain hidden until we acknowledge it and bringing it into the light of God by confessing and asking God for His forgiveness.

- It is not to believe in Jesus Christ and His finished work on the cross.

- Not believing in God the Father and the Holy Spirit.

- Through addictions in our life such as alcohol, drugs, prescription medication, marijuana, heroin, etc.

- Unforgiveness and bitterness towards someone who's hurt us is an enormous open door for the devil (Hebrews 12:15). I have heard testimonies of people who had cancer, and as soon as they genuinely forgave someone, they got healed. This is how strong unforgiveness can hold us back in life. You must have heard the saying forget the past and look to the future? We cannot change the past, and by dwelling on the past, we waste time building a better future.

- Pride and jealousy. We may think this point is not such a big deal, but through pride and jealousy, Satan was kicked out of heaven, and sin entered into the world (Isaiah 14:12-15, Ezekiel 28:12-18, Proverbs 16:18, Genesis 3:1-5).

- The love of money and power is another stronghold that usually destroys people's morality and sanity (1 Timothy 6:10). Some people will do just about anything for money. It has the potential to change a person's personality. Our motto in life should be that we rule money, and money does not rule us!

- Sexual sins with partners other than one's legal husband or wife (1 Corinthians 6:18).

- Lust, resulting in sexual sins against children, the act of rape, sex with a prostitute, and same-sex relationships. God is clear that those involved in sexual immorality will not inherit the kingdom of God. 1 Corinthians 6:9-10 says this, *'Or do you not know that the unrighteous will not inherit the kingdom of God? Do not be deceived: neither the sexually immoral, nor idolaters, nor adulterers, nor men who practice homosexuality, nor sodomites, nor thieves, nor covetous, nor drunkards, nor revilers, nor extortioners will inherit the kingdom of God."*

- Through watching sexually perverse scenes and pornography.

- Watching horror movies or demonically inspired movies.

- Listening to heavy metal music with lyrics of profanity, murder, suicide, etc. (Proverbs 18:21, Ephesians 4:29, Matthew 15:11).

- Rebellion and stubbornness. The prophet Samuel compared rebellion to the sin of witchcraft and stubbornness to iniquity and idolatry (1 Samuel 15:23).

- Experiencing extreme anger or fear caused by a situation where we do not control our emotions (Ephesians 4:26-28).

- Praying to other gods and objects that are not our Creator - God the Father, God the Son, and God the Holy Spirit (Exodus 20:2-5).

- Not honouring our parents. There is a curse on a person's life if they do not honour their parents. According to biblical standards, honouring our parents means being thankful for all they have done for us, obeying them when you are young, loving them, and caring for them in their old age (Deuteronomy 27:15). Of course, a Christian child cannot respect or obey a parent that is a witch or warlock for Satan. In this case, I would say we need to acknowledge them as our earthly father and mother but to pray that God will save them from the clutches of Satan. Our Heavenly Father should be honoured as our first parent, though, before our earthly parents. My book *Clothed for the King* explains in detail how God is our primary parent.

- Anti-Semitism. This act is hating the Jews and Israel, which is Jesus' beloved nation. Jesus himself was born into a Jewish family, and Satan has always been against the Jewish nation for that reason. In Genesis 12:3, God said to Israel, *"I will bless those who bless you, and whoever curses you I will curse, and all peoples on earth will be blessed through you."* Therefore, if you hate the Jews, you are cursed by God. Christians not born a Jew are Gentiles and became Spiritual Jews through the reconciliation of Jesus' crucifixion (Ephesians 2:11-14).

- By lying and deceiving. God said in Proverbs 12:22 that lying lips are an abomination to Him, but those who act faithfully are His delight. A person who lies belongs to the devil, who is their father (John 8:44).

- Accursed things you have invited into your home like objects, images, books, people, etc.

- Through occult activities, people open the door very wide to invite the demons into their bodies. In Mark 5, Jesus restored a demon-possessed man by commanding the unclean spirit to come out of him. Jesus asked the unclean spirit what his name was, and he responded, 'My name is Legion, for we are many'. This is an example of how a ruler demon with his sub-ruler demons went into the man's body to control him. Even Luke 8:2 referred to Mary called Magdalene, who was healed of evil spirits and infirmities. This same Mary Magdalene was a disciple of Jesus. According to the Gospel accounts, Jesus cleansed her of seven demons. She was one of the witnesses of the crucifixion and burial of Jesus, and famously, was the first person to see Him after His resurrection. Demons enter a body to do their damaging works. They may work through some of our family members, friends, and trustworthy men and women in society. Those who we love and trust the most are how Satan sometimes comes to us to destroy us. These people may not even realise they are demon-possessed or listening to the devil. That is why we have to recognize him if he comes through them so that we can resist him! In 2 Corinthians 11, the apostle Paul taught the church how to be aware of false apostles and deceitful workers who transform themselves into apostles of Christ.

Some Well-known Occult Activities

Fortune Telling	Paranormal phenomena
Black or White Magic	Talking to the dead
Tarot card readings	Playing with Ouija boards
Spiritism	Seeking after ghosts
Horoscopes	Dabbling in occult practices
Psychics	Occult and witches studies
Mediums	Astrology and numerology
Séances	Member of an occult organization
Witchery	Casting spells
Sorcery	Satanism
Astrology	Demon worship
Wicca	Voodoo, and many more

Being involved in occult activities is like placing a 'vacancy' sign on your life for evil spirits to enter. That is how the enemy begins to build brick-by-brick till it becomes a wall. This wall is then hard to break down on our own without the help of God. 2 Corinthians 4:4 says, *"The god of this age (a reference to Satan) has blinded the minds of unbelievers so that they cannot see the light of the gospel that displays the glory of Christ, who is the image of God."* If that is the devil's strategy in those who haven't trusted in Christ, how is he working in the lives of those who have trusted in the Lord? His purpose is usually to confuse, frustrate, and even steal the truth of God that has been deposited into their hearts.

The first big sign we look for if we want to discern which demon/s are ruling a person or situation is to recognize one or more of the above examples.

Other things to look for are:

- Bad things keep happening to a person.
- An illness that the doctors cannot cure. Or the same disease is running in the family.
- The same problem runs in the family line, for example, alcoholism, dying at a young age, or divorce.
- Family members keep ending up in jail.
- Rebellious children.
- Poverty, etc.

The best thing to do in any of these cases is to visit a Church or preacher specializing in deliverance to help you get rid of the demon/s or curses. Make sure you ask the right person to help you with deliverance and measure their actions with what the Bible teaches us. Look for real-life testimonies where God was working through the deliverer. They need to declare Jesus Christ as their Lord. But the most critical sign you need to look for is that this person believes and operates under the same ministry and characteristics as Jesus Christ worked when He was on this earth.

The simplest way of getting rid of a demon/s in one's life is to demand them in an audible voice to leave in the Name of Jesus Christ. Some ruler demons are so strong and will only go through prayer and fasting (Mark 9:29).

Deliverance

In Christianity, deliverance is done through prayers and no other funny business. When working in an office with a few team members, I shared the Gospel with a colleague who went through devastating stuff and illness. She then mentioned that a friend invited her to go overseas to a so-called healer who did operations with his bare hands. Almost like digging his fingers and hands into the body as you would press your hands into a ball of bread dough.

I was shocked when I heard this, and the most shocking part was that as a Christian believer, she was considering it because he has done it in the name of God! The Only True God *(God the Father, Jesus Christ, Holy Spirit)* will never heal a person like that. Throughout Jesus' ministry on earth, as mentioned in the Bible, He only had to say the words 'be healed', and the person got healed. This is how we have to discern if something is not of God! Clearly, this was a demonic act! Just thinking of the hygiene standards, I wonder how many people lived after the so-called healing operations? Or what may have taken place spiritually?

The good news is that the devil or a demon cannot own a born again Christian because he/she belongs to God unless they start taking part in demonic activities, which will change their status of being Spirit-filled or born again. We have to realize that a born again Christian can be under demonic oppression or control. If we acknowledge this can happen and safeguard ourselves from that, we have won most of the battle. But if we think we are safe and the devil and his demons cannot influence or hurt us, we have fallen for the lie. No person on this earth is a hundred per cent protected from the devil and his demons. That is why we always have to be on our guard to recognize when and where they are trying to infiltrate our lives.

Deliverance prayers, now and then, are great tools to protect oneself. We have to regularly break any possible curses in the Name of Jesus Christ. There are many evil people in this world, and sometimes we even speak a curse over our own life without realizing it. I used to ask a family member how he was going, and he usually answered in a joke, 'still poor and getting old'. It took a few years to make him aware of the curse he was putting on himself each time. When I was younger, people gave me compliments, and I never knew how to handle it. I used to explain why I was not as good as they said until I learned about cursing oneself. The best thing to do is to say 'thank you for the compliment or thank you for the kind words' and leave it at that.

Christians can clean and heal themselves from demons and curses. They do not always have to visit a deliverer because it's through the power of Jesus Christ, a deliverer receives the victory, not through their own doing. If a person prays directly to Jesus Christ for help to deliver them, it can happen in one's privacy. But if there is no success, the person requires a deliverer that moves and operates in the power of the Holy Spirit. In Matthew 16:19, Jesus said to Peter, *"I will give you the keys of the kingdom of heaven; whatever you bind on earth will be bound in heaven, and whatever you loose on earth will be loosed in heaven."*

How do we bind a demon or break a curse over ourselves? Start by praying and worshipping, which invites Jesus and the Holy Spirit into the deliverance session. Always ask the Holy Spirit for guidance and He will direct your deliverance prayer. Use the Word of God and the name of Jesus Christ to bind demon/s and breaking the curse/s over yourself. For example, you'll say out loud:

"Jealousy demon that is in me or around me. I bind you in the Name of Jesus Christ, my Lord and Saviour. You have no power or authority over me because Jesus bought me with His blood. I belong to Him and I command you, jealousy demon, to leave me now in Jesus Christ's name. I ask you, Holy Spirit, who is my comforter, to protect me from the devil and his demons. I give my life to You to guide me in your righteous ways. I pray this in Jesus Christ Name. Amen and Amen!"

In Luke 10, Jesus sent out seventy-two other disciples to go ahead to the different towns He would later visit. They returned with joy, saying to Him, 'Even the demons submit to us in Your name'. Then Jesus answered them in verses 18-20, *"I saw Satan fall like lightning from heaven. I have given you authority to trample on snakes and scorpions and to overcome all the power of the enemy; nothing will harm you. However, do not rejoice that the spirits submit to you, but rejoice that your names are written in heaven."*

How do we cast a demon out of our body? Again in the name of Jesus Christ. Jesus had the authority of God and is The Righteous One. Mark 1:21-25 describes when Jesus went to Capernaum and was teaching in the synagogue on the Sabbath. A man was possessed by an impure spirit and cried out, *"What do you want with us, Jesus of Nazareth? Have you come to destroy us? I know who you are, the Holy One of God!"* Jesus said sternly, *"Be quiet! Come out of him!"* The impure spirit shook the man violently and came out of him with a shriek.

Jesus' victory on the cross gave us the authority to cast demons out in His NAME. In Matthew 10:8, Jesus told His disciples, *"Heal the sick, cleanse the lepers, raise the dead, cast out devils: freely ye have received, freely give."* When you cast a demon out, you'll start with prayer and worship again to prepare the atmosphere, inviting Jesus and the Holy Spirit into your session. Also, pray for guidance. You can say something like this:

"Jesus, thank you that You died for me on the cross, to save my soul and heal my body. 1 Peter 2:24 says that You bore my sins on the cross, and by Your wounds, I am healed. Addiction demon (name the specific addiction you struggle with), I demand you in the Name of Jesus Christ to leave my body now, and I bind all your destructive work in me, in the Name of Jesus Christ, my Lord and Saviour! You have no right over my children in the Name of Jesus Christ, and you'll not make your resting place at them. I ask Jesus Christ to send you to the place where He wants you to go, until Judgement Day. You, addiction demon, will not bother my family or me ever again, in the Name of Jesus Christ. I now invite God's sovereign Holy Spirit to come and live inside of me and fill the spot where the demon/s occupied. I pray this in Jesus Christ's great Name. Amen and Amen!"

Jesus said in John 12:12-14, *"Very truly I tell you, whoever believes in me will do the works I have been doing, and they will do even greater things than these because I am going to the Father. And I will do whatever you ask in My name, so that the Father may be glorified in the Son. You may ask me for anything in My name, and I will do it."*

It is important to remember that we have to invite the Holy Spirit to come into our body after a demon was cast out. To fill us with His healing and protection. A person who has doors still open to the devil or the demonic must not get involved in deliverance by themselves. If a person keeps the door open, the demon/s can come back and bring seven worse than themselves to live in the person again. We do not want to be worse off than before, as Jesus taught in Matthew 12:43-45. After deliverance, close all doors opened to the demonic earlier, and do not operate in the sin anymore. In John 5, after Jesus healed the blind, lame, and paralyzed man at the pool of Bethesda, He saw him later at the temple and said to the man, *"See, you are well again. Stop sinning or something worse may happen to you."*

It is crucial that a person first wants to get delivered and then have a support system that will help them stand firm and keep strong against that weakness in their life. Of course, Jesus is there for everyone who calls on His Name and believes that He can help them been delivered from the devil's oppression and stay healthy. Sometimes the hold of the demon/s can be so strong that the person needs help from another spiritually strong believer.

Pray the following 'Deliverance Prayer' out loud. And if you can do it together with a family member or friend, it will work even better, as God's Word promise us in Matthew 18:20, *"For where two or three are gathered together in my name, there am I in the midst of them"*.

Deliverance Prayer in General

> *Dear Jesus,*
>
> *Thank you for your protection against my enemies in this world (The devil and his demons).*
>
> *Jesus, just as the seventy-two disciples in Luke 10:17, returned with joy and said, "Lord, even the demons submit to us in your name." I am praising You that the demons oppressing me now will submit and flee from me in Your Name. Jesus, please release a legion of your strongest warrior angels to assist me and protect me now and in the weeks to come after my deliverance. I speak the blood of Jesus Christ over me, my family, my house, my work, and my car, which will protect me against every devil and demon.*
>
> *Right now, I bind and rebuke every demon and unclean spirit working inside and against me, in the Name of Jesus Christ. I bind all hindering spirits from interfering with my deliverance in the Name of Jesus Christ. I rebuke any strongman now, in and around me, in the Name of Jesus Christ.*
>
> *I invite the Holy Spirit to come and live in me now, and I ask that the Holy Spirit will cut off all demons and their strongmen with His two-edged sword and release me from every unclean spirit.*
>
> *I bind every demon leaving my body and my life now in the Name of Jesus Christ and send them to go where Jesus Christ is sending them until Judgement Day. I pray that the Holy Spirit will talk to me now and guide me in which demons I need to bind in the Name of Jesus Christ. Holy Spirit, make my senses sensitive to Your Voice.*

I bind every spirit of addiction, whether food, alcohol, drugs or smoking.

I bind the spirits of any sickness, infirmity or disease, poverty, depression, anger, or sexual sin, in and around me in the Name of Jesus Christ. I declare that these demons that leave me now have no legal right to operate in my body or life anymore, in the Name of Jesus Christ. I break and bind any unforgiveness in me, in the Name of Jesus Christ.

If there is any demon or strongman left inside me, I demand you to leave my body now in the Name of Jesus Christ. As every demon and strongman comes out of me, you are ordered in Jesus Christ's Name to go where He sends you and never return to earth or any person until your judgement day.

I seal my deliverance with the blood of Jesus Christ. I am totally and completely free from any unclean spirit or demon operating in my body and life. I will never be bothered by these demons again, in the Name of Jesus Christ.

God our Father, Jesus Christ, and wonderful Holy Spirit, who is with me every day, thank you for your protection against all evil as my life continues. Please teach and guide me in your perfect way, my Lord, so that I can be spiritually strong against every evil that comes against me and that I reach the full potential of that which You have created me to be.

I love you, Lord, and I thank you for my perfect deliverance now in Jesus Christ's Wonderful Name.

Amen and Amen!

The Two Houses That Demons Can Occupy

There are two houses in our life that we need to keep clean from satanic invasion to have a more peaceful life. One is our human body which houses our spirit, soul, and the Holy Spirit (of those born again). The second is the physical house that we live in here on earth. As already discussed in the previous passages, the doors that demons can move into our body are through our eyes, ears, smell and taste, mind, and sexual activities. The ways we open doors for evil spirits into our physical home are through the following:

- Bringing physical things into our home dedicated to Satan like charms, crystals, dream catchers, occult or demonic inspired books, ornaments and images representing foreign gods such as Buddhas etc.

- Doing occult activities in the home such as playing with Ouija boards, seeking ghosts, doing tarot card readings, satan or demon worshipping, worshipping foreign gods, etc.

- Immoral sexual practices that took place inside the house through physical actions, watching pornography, etc.

- Inviting satan and demons in deliberately.

- A murder or suicide that took place inside the house.

- By watching horror and satanically inspired movies or television shows.

- Inviting the wrong crowd or person into our home.

- Cursed objects that may have entered the home consciously or unconsciously. For example, someone may have consciously cursed an item, given it to another person as a gift, or planted it inside the house. An unfortunate situation is when someone bought a gift for someone else, not knowing it was cursed. For example, Buddha or other prayer ornaments, traditional or voodoo dolls, wrist bands, or necklaces made from traditional beads that are cursed. Sometimes we also buy cursed objects and are not aware of them. It's an excellent practice to bless everything you bring into your house in the Name of Jesus Christ, to break any curses. Other times, evil people who want to curse someone will give them an expensive precious gift, which they have cursed. Just remember, obvious things dedicated to Satan like Buddha ornaments, dream catchers, and demonically inspired books cannot be blessed in Jesus Christ's name. It is unclean to start with and will always stay unclean of the association.

That is why we bless our food before we eat it! In Mark 16:17-18, Jesus said, *"And these signs will accompany those who believe: In my name, they will drive out demons; they will speak in new tongues; they will pick up snakes with their hands; and when they drink deadly poison, it will not hurt them at all; they will place their hands on sick people, and they will get well."* This verse is not an invitation to pick up snakes or drink poison to see how far God's protection stretches! Remember when Jesus fasted for forty days and forty nights in the wilderness, Satan said to Him, if He is the Son of God, to throw himself down from the temple because it is written that God will command His angels to lift Him up. That is when Jesus said it is also written not to put the Lord God to the test.

The Jezebel, Religious, and Antichrist Spirits

The Jezebel Spirit:

A quote from Michael Bradley on the Jezebel Spirit: "Without question, the nastiest, evil, most disgusting, cunning, and seductive spirit in Satan's hierarchy has to be what many call the Jezebel spirit."

For decades my family has been pestered, and in some cases, are still bothered by demonic attacks. Decades of praying and begging God on their behalf brought no success. At one stage, my family's issues affected me so profoundly that I questioned God's authority, might, and power. I've made known to God how I felt. I knew people need to give the first step, and God will do the rest, but I could not understand why my prayers were not answered over that long period. One day I was at a breaking point when God spoke to my heart, saying: 'Follow Me and leave your family to Me!' I said to God, 'Okay, I'll follow You, and will trust that You'll let me see them in heaven one day'. It was tough for me to do this because I was always trying to fix things myself. I wanted to see results quickly because I was exhausted from dealing with all the issues. I desired love and peace in my life. Often, the devil keeps us so busy with family problems that we do not have enough time to follow God properly, and God needs to be our first priority. After this big decision, I found I had more time to spend learning about God and the Bible, and my life became more peaceful and joyful. After a few years, I started to see some of the same traits beginning to manifest in my children's lives.

I talked to God earnestly and asked Him, 'Why is it that my prayers over decades could not help my family? Is it because I'm praying wrongly, or something I am doing wrong, or is it because of their rebellious hearts?' I said, 'I do not know if I can handle it again if my adult children bring the same problems into my life again.' Then God spoke to my heart and said, 'Drive up the mountain, and go and bind the Jezebel Spirit over your city, over your family, and your children.' I did not obey this message the first time because I thought maybe it was just my thoughts. The issues in my children's lives did not resolve. A couple of months later, I was crying out to God again with the same complaints. Again, He spoke to my heart the same message.

I thought, okay God, maybe it was Your voice that I heard the first time and ignored. So I drove up the mountain, which is about half an hour's drive from my home. I prayed over my city and children, and I bound the Jezebel Spirit in Jesus Christ's Name over my city, over my family, over my husband and me, and my children. I also threw a few painted river stones with Bible verses down the mountain. Amazingly when I got home, I could already feel there was a shift in the atmosphere, and there was an instant change in my children's issues. Out of experience, I agree with Michael

Bradley's statement that the Jezebel Spirit is one of the nastiest evil spirits in Satan's hierarchy, apart from the Religious Spirit and the Antichrist Spirit, which I'll also touch on briefly.

The Jezebel Spirit always wants to manipulate and dominate. She is one of the ruler spirits with many sub and sub-sub rulers under her. She usually controls women but can also control men. 'Dominate' is a satanic word because God never dominates! God gave us all free will to choose if we want to serve Him or not. He will never force or control us. Where you encounter domination, somewhere behind it is Satan. His ambition, desire and strategy; is to come to the point where he dominates the entire world, but he will dominate with a system of darkness. God's Kingdom is a kingdom of light, and Satan's kingdom is one of darkness. Those in God's Kingdom know whom they are serving, and they see what they are doing. Most in Satan's kingdom do not even know why they are serving him, nor do they know what they are doing. Jezebel usually seduces a person through the lusts of the flesh to carry out her plan to kill, steal, and destroy.

Characteristics of the Jezebel Spirit:

- Isolation.
- Confusion.
- Insecurity.
- Huge ego.
- Rebellion.
- Narcissism.
- Know it all.
- Is vengeful.
- Power-driven.
- Undisciplined.

- Unreasonable.
- Is unforgiving.
- Money hungry.
- Lies and deceit.
- Is very ambitious.
- Lack of empathy.
- Suicidal thoughts.
- Sexually immoral.
- Pride and arrogance.
- Criticizing everyone.
- Commands attention.
- Falsely accusing others.
- Tends to be oversensitive.
- Are irritable and aggressive.
- Taking credit for everything.
- Pretends to be very religious.
- Having issues of fear and rejection.
- Usually oppresses and bullies others.
- Wants to dominate situations and others.
- Gives a front of being charming and sweet.
- Fails to conform to social norms and want their ways.
- Plays the victim, is never wrong, and blames everyone else.

- A sociopath who is antisocial and disregards the rights of others.

- Don't want to hear about God, Jesus Christ, or the Holy Spirit.

- Attempts to make you look like the problem or a Jezebel.

The Religious Spirit:

A religious spirit is a demonic spirit that influences a person, or group of people, to replace a genuine relationship with God. When people operate out of a religious spirit, they attempt to earn salvation themselves, ignoring the work that Jesus has done on the cross. Ephesians 2:8-9 says, *"For it is by grace you have been saved through faith, and that not of yourselves; it is the gift of God, not by works, lest anyone should boast."* This evil spirit has established nonbiblical beliefs and customs for generations. We shouldn't ignore the work of the religious spirit. It's waiting for an open door to enter and cause judgement and destruction amongst believers and the Church.

Jesus was giving orders to His disciples in Mark 8:15, saying watch out, beware of the leaven of the Pharisees, and the leaven of Herod. The leaven of the Pharisees refers to the Religious Spirit. The leaven of Herod is referring to the Political Spirit. There is a form of godliness that goes with the Religious Spirit, but it has no Godly power. For example, the Kingdom of God is about relationships, whereas religion is about systems. The Kingdom of God is about being with God, hanging with Him, and eating from the Tree of Life. The Religious Spirit is about knowledge. What you know, how you can control things through knowledge and understanding.

Another point is that the Kingdom of God is our walk with God. It's all about living as the Holy Spirit leads us. Where again, the Religious Spirit likes to get all cosy in structures. There is nothing wrong with structures that God has put into place, but some that people try to live under is because they like the control they have with their understanding and carnal soul. Living inside those structures makes them feel good. All religions are based on that principle where it is from the carnal rule of man. Adam and Eve sold their birthright of being with God, having a relationship, enjoying His presence forever, then went into a system. Because they ate from the tree of knowledge of good and evil, they tried to work out what is good and evil. Religion is based on determining what is good. Religion also says here are the rules for good, try to obey them, and here are the rules for evil, so try and stay away from them. It is all about man's rules or laws versus God's laws. Religion is what people do to justify themselves before God. It is work and bragging about how good 'you' are.

People that usually get caught up in a religious spirit have started with the right heart but later wonder what is wrong. They no longer feel free but feel confined. This issue is what Paul describes in 2 Corinthians 3:6 when he says, '...for the letter *(knowledge)* kills, but the Spirit *(Holy Spirit)* gives life'. Jesus said in Matthew 11:28-30, *"Come to Me, all you who labour and are heavy laden, and I will give you rest. Take My yoke upon you and learn from Me, for I am gentle and lowly in heart, and you will find rest for your souls. For My yoke is easy, and My burden is light."* Break with religion and tradition, and follow Jesus to truly feel the peace and freedom you were born to experience with God!

Characteristics of the Religious Spirit:

- Judging others and thinking themselves holy.

- Always critical of other people's walk with God.

- Judging other people by their appearance.

- Trying to earn God's love and salvation through good works instead of trusting Christ for their salvation.

- Regularly arguing about the Bible instead of building and learning from each other.

- Desire position and honour in the church more than recognition from God.

- Perform Christian duties, but have no passion or hunger for God.

- Trying to conform to outward holiness without inward transformation.

The Antichrist Spirit:

The word antichrist means a person or force seen as opposing Christ or the Christian Church. The Antichrist with a capital 'A' is the person yet to be revealed at the end of this age when the seven-year tribulation will take place on earth. It means standing in place of Christ and wants to be worshipped as God. He will be the main enemy of Jesus Christ, expected to rule the world until Jesus Christ's *Second Coming* to earth. Satan is the leading Antichrist spirit who will control this person, ruling the world during the tribulation period, and his primary target is to destroy Jesus Christ and Christianity. Read more about the Antichrist in Chapter 6 - *The Rapture, Tribulation, And the Return of Christ.*

The antichrist spirit existed from the time of Jesus Christ's first coming. In 1 John 2:18, John wrote, *"Little children, it is the last hour; and as you have heard that the Antichrist is coming, even now many antichrists have come, by which we know that it is the last hour."*

Men like Adolf Hitler, Antiochus Epiphanes etc., were all empowered and controlled by the antichrist spirit; in other words, Satan ruled through them. Today, any person against Jesus Christ, the Word of God, or anything Godly, is under the antichrist spirit.

In 1 John 4:1-3, we read, *"Dear friends, do not believe every spirit, but test the spirits to see whether they are from God because many false prophets have gone out into the world. This is how you can recognize the Spirit of God: Every spirit that acknowledges that Jesus Christ has come in the flesh is from God, but every spirit that does not acknowledge Jesus is not from God. This is the spirit of the antichrist, which you have heard is coming and even now is already in the world."*

Characteristics of the Antichrist Spirit:

- Denies, perverts or twists the truth about Jesus and that He is God. He was a man when He was on earth *(He had flesh)*. He died and rose from the dead physically. He denies that

Salvation is only by grace through faith. Is against the Jews and working to wipe them from the earth. Denies that Jesus is alive and will come back to rule the world for all eternity.

- Denial of the validity of God's Word.

- Denial of Christ's Lordship.

- Persecutes God's people.

- He is a master of deception.

- Uses violence to accomplish his purposes.

- Hates the family unit that God created and wants to destroy it at all cost.

- The spirit of the antichrist twists Christian doctrine to confuse the Church.

- The Holy Spirit clearly says that in later times some will abandon the faith and follow deceiving spirits and things taught by demons, called the great apostasy (1 Timothy 4:1).

Why must we desire to be infilled with God's Holy Spirit? The Holy Spirit is the Third Divine Person of the Trinity (Matthew 28:19). He is omnipresent and connects us directly with God our Father and Jesus Christ (Matthew 28:19, Psalm 139:71-10, Ephesians 2:18). Jesus said in John 14:21, *"Whoever has my commandments and keeps them is the one who loves me, and the one who loves me will be loved by my Father, and I too will love them and show myself to them."*

The Holy Spirit also helps us with the following:

- He prays for us (Romans 8:26).

- He convicts us of sin (John 16:8).

- He gives us wisdom (Isaiah 11:2).

- He helps us to pray (Romans 8:26).

- Gives us inner strength (Ephesians 3:16).

- He gives us Spiritual Gifts (1 Corinthians 12:1-11).
- He helps us to discern spirits (1 Corinthians 12:10).
- He frees us from the power of sin (Romans 8:2).
- He gives us the power to be witnesses of Jesus (Acts 1:8).
- He identifies and seals us as God's own (Ephesians 1:13).
- Teach and testifies to us about God our Father, and Jesus Christ (John 14:26, John 15:26).
- Speaks to us and guides us daily (Revelation 2:7, John 16:13).
- Reveals God's secrets and the future to us (1 Corinthians 2:10).
- Encourages us, filling us with boldness (Acts 9:31, Acts 4:31).
- He confirms things as true because He is the Spirit of Truth (Romans 9:1, John 14:17).
- He gives us personal instructions to protect and guide us (Acts 8:29).
- He transforms us more and more into the image of Jesus (2 Corinthians 3:18).
- He produces fruit in our lives, like love, joy, peace, patience, kindness, goodness, faithfulness, gentleness, and self-control (Galatians 5:22-23).
- He calls for the return of Jesus so that our hearts also cries out (Revelation 22:17).
- Scripture shows that the Holy Spirit is God (Acts 5:3-5).

In Matthew 16:13-16, when Jesus came to the region of Caesarea Philippi, He asked His disciples, *"Who do people say the Son of Man is?"* They replied, *"Some say John the Baptist; others say Elijah; and still others, Jeremiah or one of the prophets." Jesus* then asked them: *"Who do you say I am?"*

Simon Peter answered, *"You are the Messiah, the Son of the living God."*

Jesus replied, *"Blessed are you, Simon son of Jonah, for this was not revealed to you by flesh and blood, but by my Father in heaven. And I tell you that you are Peter, and on this rock, I will build my church, and the gates of Hades will not overcome it. I will give you the keys of the kingdom of heaven; whatever you bind on earth will be bound in heaven, and whatever you loose on earth will be loosed in heaven."*

There are a few revelations we can take from the above Scripture. Firstly, it is an excellent example of how the Holy Spirit revealed to Simon Peter that Jesus is the Messiah and Son of the Living God! Secondly, the true Church on earth will be led by the Holy Spirit because Jesus said that this revelation is the rock on which He will build His Church. Thirdly, the gates of Hades *(Satan and his demons are currently dwelling in Hades)* will not overcome those who the Holy Spirit leads. Fourthly, the keys of the kingdom of heaven are given to the Spirit-filled Church that Jesus is establishing on earth, meaning that they can bind the devil's works and lose the blessings of God from heaven. Fifthly, the words 'Son of the **living God**' refers to God who is alive and not a man-made god, which is an object that is dead.

CHAPTER 5

HEAR GOD SPEAK

Humanity is desperate to hear God speaking to them. No wonder they are seeking after all the unbiblical ways such as dabbling in the occult, following new age movements, visiting psychics, playing with Ouija boards, etc. They do not know how available God is.

Following are the ways God speak to us:

- First and foremost, by His Word *(the Bible)*.

- Visions and dreams.

- Signs and wonders.

- Through our circumstances.

- As the still small voice of the indwelling Holy Spirit.

- With an audible voice, but only some will experience God this way.

- By His Prophets, those over the centuries and the ones still alive.

- Through Godly preachers, pastors, evangelists, anointed people, family, and friends.

- God may even use an unbeliever to get through to us if other ways do not work.

The closer our walk with God, the clearer His voice becomes. In John 10:27, Jesus said, *"My sheep hear My voice, and I know them, and they follow Me."* Therefore, through a relationship with God, we'll recognise His voice. If I come to your house today and ask to enter, your first reaction would be 'Who are you?'. If I kept insisting on being let in, you would most probably call the police to remove me. If you know me, it's another story because you'll let me in straight away. In John 17:3, Jesus said, *"Now this is eternal life: that they know You, the only true God, and Jesus Christ, whom You have sent."*

To recognise God's voice, we must belong to Him. We hear His voice when we spend time in Bible study. When thoughts recur, pray about them to discern if they are coming from God. Keep in mind; God will never give you a message that contradicts the Bible. Although God can manifest in a supernatural way, like when He spoke to Moses through a burning bush, His speech is usually gentle and meek. Gentleness implies being merciful and self-controlled. Meekness is not weakness. It means to be humble, patient but with strength under control. In 2 Corinthians 10:1, the apostle Paul said, *"Now I, myself, urge you by the meekness and gentleness of Christ."* In Galatians 5:22-23, we read, *"But the fruit of the Spirit is love, joy, peace, patience, kindness, goodness, faithfulness, gentleness, self-control; against such things, there is no law."*

I usually enjoy listening to preachers of the Word who sound enthusiastic and energetic. Their voice must have character and not a monotone, but my spirit resists everything they say as soon as they start shouting. Sometimes it is well-known preachers who give great messages. Apart from the above Scriptures telling us about Jesus and the Holy Spirit's gentleness, there are many more in the Bible. This characteristic makes it much easier for us to recognize their voices amongst the loud voices of the world.

I want to detail 'visions and dreams' because this is a fundamental way God speaks to us. The world has become so busy that we may miss God's voice during the day, and the only way He can get our attention is when the world has calmed down and our bodies are at rest. I have never really dreamt, or so I thought, and when I did, I mostly could not remember it when I woke up. During 2019 I had a 'spiritual' dream that made me look into its possible meaning. The more research I did, the more I felt God was speaking to me to start interpreting my dreams. As I became more aware that God does speak to us at night, I asked Him to help me remember my dreams if He wanted me to note what He is saying to me. My dreams started to increase, and I even had two to three on some nights. Through my research, I came across a few gifted Biblical dream interpreters. Their ministries have spanned several decades. When I listened to them, I felt the anointing of God. They are John Paul Jackson, Dr Mark Virkler, Dr Charity Kayembe, James & Michal Ann Goll, Autumn Mann, and Perry Stone.

In this chapter, I'll discuss some guidelines on Biblical dream interpretations to get you started. The prophet Joel, who lived in the 9th century B.C., prophesied in Joel 2:28, *"I will pour out my Spirit on all people. Your sons and your daughters will prophesy, your old men will dream dreams, and your young men will see visions."*

The main difference between visions and dreams in the Bible is that dreams are received while sleeping. Visions are received while awake, and they are often 'in the Spirit', which means to be more conscious of spiritual things than natural things.

I mostly dream but had two visions in 2019 while I was visiting two different churches. The first was when I visited a church with my daughter when she introduced an African preacher to an Australian preacher. The service was quite intense, as the Australian preacher was very focused on spiritual warfare. I had a side vision of Jesus sitting on a white horse during the service, dressed in a red robe. His horse was standing on a hill, and He was overlooking a valley with thousands of other riders sitting on white horses. They were all dressed in white robes. They were looking at Jesus on the hill while He was looking at them. This vision gave me the sense that Jesus was gathering his troops for the final conflict before His millennial reign.

A few months after this vision, I was preaching at a small African church in Australia. During the worship session, I saw a huge black tree's roots that grew over the building, slowly shrinking as the roots disappeared. I understood from this vision that the demonic stronghold over the church and building was broken, and the dark forces had disappeared. To receive a vision is a fantastic experience because you are fully awake, and in a few seconds, you see an image playing in front of you like a video.

Visions take on more clarity than dreams. In a vision, you may taste, smell, hear sounds and are very alert to colours. It seems to be unfolding right at that moment. Dreams come at night, whereas visions occasionally happen during the day. A vision is 'in the Spirit' when God wants to attract our attention to something important. Another way to determine if a vision or dream is important is when there is a heavy pressing on your spirit. We have to be sensitive to the Holy Spirit to determine which visions and dreams are from God and need interpretation.

Dream Interpretation

We spent a third of our life sleeping, and it is this time God speaks to us in dreams. Our body sleeps during the night, but our spirit is always awake and can receive revelation from God at any time. Sleeping is also a time that our body undergoes repairing and detoxification. Poor sleeping patterns increase our risk of diseases and interfere with our REM *(rapid eye movement)* sleep at night when we are dreaming.

Sometimes, we do not remember dreams because we have not been taught their importance and how to remember them. The process of remembering is similar to how revelation embeds itself into our conscious mind. Memory is a picture, and our dreams are also pictures. By putting in the effort to learn God's language of dreams, we demonstrate our commitment and desire to deepen our intimacy with Him.

In Job 33:14-16, we read how God speaks to us at night, *'For God may speak in one way, or in another, yet man does not perceive it. In a dream, in a vision of the night, when deep sleep falls upon men while slumbering on their beds, then He opens the ears of men, and seals their instruction."*

Some dreams are demonically inspired, so, therefore, we must be vigilant to protect our dream life! When you go to bed at night, first pray the covering of Jesus Christ's blood over you and your room. Bind all attacks of Satan and his demons, and command them to leave in the name of Jesus Christ. Focus on Jesus as you fall asleep. Breathe slowly and focus on Him while repeating His name. Many times when I'm trying to fall asleep, I picture myself dancing for God the Father and Jesus Christ in heaven while listening to Christian music playing softly.

It may be some years before God grants you the meaning of some dreams. He may want to remind us that dream interpretation does not lie with us but with Him. In Genesis 40, we read that the cupbearer and the baker of the king of Egypt were in prison with Joseph. One day Joseph asked them why they look so sad. They said, *"We both had dreams, but there is no one to interpret them."* Joseph said to them, *"Do not interpretations belong to God? Tell me your dreams."* We must always depend on God. Ask the Holy Spirit to help you interpret your dreams. It does not mean to resign ourselves to passive waiting. 'Active' waiting means that through meditation, research, fellowship, reading the Bible, praying, discussing with trusted Godly advisors, and setting time aside to commune with the Holy Spirit, we prepare to receive the interpretation in God's timing. Be careful not to ask just anyone what they think your dream means because the enemy may find a foot in the door to give you the wrong message. Do not allow frustration to set in either, to rob you of the peace of God. Wait for God patiently to reveal the meaning of your dream. Also, pray that He will send the right person across your path at the right time to help interpret your dream.

Dreams are usually highly symbolic and are rarely literal. The people, places, and things in our dreams often represent something else. Just as Jesus told parables in the New Testament in a unique way, he talks to us in our dreams in a unique way. The symbols will come from a Biblical point of view and the dreamer's personal life.

Every person has their dream language with God. One thing can mean something to you, while the same thing will mean something different to another person. Christians must focus on the Biblical way of dream interpretation to receive the right message from God.

Often, the definition of names or objects will give the correct meaning or identity. Experience has shown that if you dream of a family member or a friend that dies or is in a car accident, it means precisely that. If you wake up crying or feeling upset, pray for that person immediately and ask God for His divine protection over them. Bind the spirit of death, the spirit of sickness or accident over them in the name of Jesus Christ *(whatever happened to them in the dream)*.

Biblical dream interpreters advise recording your dreams in a portfolio. Give each dream a title, and record the date. The title may reveal the meaning already. Since I started to record my dreams, I dream more. It's as if God can see that I am serious about hearing what He has to say to me, and He entrusts me with more spiritual dreams. I've had a few dreams, which I know mean something important but could not understand yet. Further on, I've explained some of my dreams and how I interpreted them.

Quick ways to record your dreams at night:

- The best way I have found is to use my smartphone because I can forward it to email when I've typed it up. I enter the title, date, and circumstances during the day when I am more awake. Once a month, I make time to print them out and file them in my dream portfolio.

- You can also keep a book and pencil next to your bed, and as soon as you wake up during the night, you can write the details down while they are still fresh in your mind. You may wake up two to three times a night to record the different dreams.

- Another way is to voice record it on your smartphone or a voice recorder; if you are not going to wake up your loved ones. Type it up at the earliest convenient time and file it in your dream portfolio.

Steps to follow when you record your dreams:

STEP 1 - Give your dream a title.

STEP 2 - Write down the date you had the dream.

STEP 3 - Record the emotion/s you experienced straight after you woke up. Were you happy, sad, anxious, angry, hurt, overwhelmed, confused, fearful, relieved, excited, burdened, felt rejected, felt loved, or surprised?

STEP 4 - Write down a short description of your circumstances. For example, My child became sick, I quarrelled with my best friend during the day, I got the news that my sibling is moving overseas.

STEP 5 - Describe the dream in as much detail as you can remember. Write down specifics like names, places, colours, objects, people *(male, female, child, grandpa, grandma, dad, mum, uncle, aunt, cousin, brother, sister, best friend, friend, doctor, teacher, etc.)*, animals *(what kind of animal)*, numbers, way of travelling *(plane, car, motorcycle, bicycle, air balloon, ship, boat, train)*.

STEP 6 - Leave enough space to write down possible meanings of the names, objects, etc. Some dreams may take months to years to figure out, and when you look through it on different occasions, you may understand some sections better because you've already written down some meanings.

Following is a short dream of mine in the proposed template:

Dream Title: **Lunch with a Friend**

Date	1ˢᵗ March 2020
Emotion	I felt loved and admired. I also felt attracted.
Circumstances	I was peaceful and happy.
Dream Description	I dreamt I was having lunch with a man who was my friend. He was attractive, and I enjoyed his company. We were sitting at a table in a cafè or restaurant, which had a white tablecloth over it. I cannot recall if I saw that the man was eating anything, but I ate a white slice of bread with butter. When we finished, I said I enjoyed his company, and we must do it again. I asked him to excuse me for a moment as I needed to go to the ladies before leaving. Then I woke up.
Possible Meaning	In the Bible, Jesus refers to Himself as our friend (John 15:12-15). Jesus is beautiful at heart and attractive because He is God, and when we are connected to Him through the Holy Spirit, we feel attracted to Him. Jesus loves us very much (John 15:9), and that is why I felt loved and admired. I was eating bread, which was a reference to Jesus feeding me the 'bread of life'. Jesus said to His disciples in John 6:35 - *"I am the bread of life; whoever comes to me shall not hunger, and whoever believes in me shall never thirst."* In this dream, Jesus was feeding me bread, which is a reference to Himself. In other words, He is teaching me His Word (Bible) and helping me to grow spiritually. The white tablecloth represents righteousness and holiness. So Jesus is teaching me the Word of God from a place of righteousness and holiness. The butter may mean Jesus gives me more than just teaching, for example, an extra anointing or spiritual gift.

How do you know if a dream is about you?

- You are observing yourself in the dream.

- If everything revolves around you, you are the principal actor, and the dream speaks to you.

- Occasionally you can shift positions from observer to participant in the dream, which means the dream is about you and others.

- Dr Mark Virkler believes that 5% of our dreams are about others and the rest about us.

When is a dream not about you but someone else?

- If you do not appear in the dream.

- If you are an observer in the dream, it's not about you. Pay attention to the things observed.

- When you are a participant in the dream, but not the centre of attention, it's partially about you. Others may be equally or more involved than you in the dream.

- Establish the sub-focuses in the dream. There are usually 2-4 sub-focuses. Sub-focuses are elements that are necessary to find the theme of the dream. Often when we remove the sub-focuses or details, the dream becomes clear. Sub-focuses are to fill the dream and have no importance on their own.

Questions to ask yourself when approaching the dream:

- What were my emotions? In what area of my life was I experiencing a similar feeling or reaction? What issue was I dealing with the day before I had the dream?

- What was I doing? The key action?

- What is God presently dealing with in my life?

- What colour was the dream, full colour, muted colours, or black and white? Colours represent specific meanings and purposes.

- What was the colour of certain symbols in the dream? For example: Was it a red or yellow car? Was it a blue or white shirt? Was it a white or black horse?

A few tips to help you remember your dreams:

- Get enough sleep during the night. Seven to nine hours of sleep per night are considered healthy and gives your body enough stamina to wake up and remember your dreams.

- Ask the Holy Spirit to wake you early in the mornings. Establish a habit of getting up at a pre-determined time. An alarm clock that suddenly wakes you up may cause you to forget your dream. For some, the alarm clock creates a negative response first thing in our day.

- Set your alarm clock for the latest time you need to get up and still make it in time for work if you go back to sleep after you initially woke up. It usually takes twenty-one days to establish a new habit.

- Between 4-6 am is usually the best time to get up, as most dreams finish around that time.

- Immediately write down any dreams when you wake up.

Things to be careful of when interpreting dreams:

- Never make a significant decision in your life based on a dream without receiving additional confirmation from God through other ways that He speaks to us.

- Do not share your dream with just anybody, but be selective with whom you share God's intimate communication. Matthew 7:6 says, *"Do not give dogs what is sacred; do not throw your pearls to pigs. If you do, they may trample them under their feet and turn and tear you to pieces."* Always wait for the Holy Spirit first to help you interpret.

Our Beloved *(Jesus)* knocks on the door of our hearts while we sleep. He longs for that intimate communion with us for which we were created. In the Song of Solomon 5:2, we read, *"I slept but my heart was awake. Listen! My beloved is knocking...."*

Every time we see a dream playing out in our life, it will encourage us, and we'll become more confident. We'll feel so loved by our God, who speaks to us and guides us. The spirit realm is all around us. Everyone would be able to hear God's voice if they were interested in listening to Him. The more we listen, the more we'll hear. The more we look, the more we'll see.

Categories of dreams:

Following is a list of twenty dream categories that can help you determine what your dream is about. God speaks to us many times, but sometimes, it is just our mind sorting out issues. Dreams can also overlap in the following categories.

1. Flushing dreams

- These dreams cleanse us of day-to-day encounters that defile us spiritually.
- A cleansing from something that may have come through the 'eye gate'. For example, watching horror movies, etc.
- If you are an observer in the dream, it's not a flushing dream.

2. Healing dreams

- These are dreams that heal us from broken relationships.
- Our opinions of others can be changed.
- In this type of dream, we are released to forgive another and see them from God's perspective.

3. Warning dreams

- Warns the dreamer not to do certain things. In Genesis 20:3, God warned Abimelek in a dream not to marry Sarah because she was a married woman.
- You can have repetitive warning dreams that seem different yet are about the same warning.

4. Calling dreams

- You may dream of an experience that will occur in the future.
- In the calling dream, you are doing something that reveals a vocation or anointing.

5. Body dreams

- These dreams may come as a result of physical sickness.
- They may also come in the last trimester of pregnancy. While your dreams may not affect the baby, your physical reactions do! Stress causes hormones to be released and your muscles to tense, etc. Your baby can feel that but does not know what you are dreaming.
- After about seven months of growth in the womb, a baby starts dreaming too.

6. Chemical dreams

- They are dreams induced by drugs, including alcohol and food. The drugs may be prescription, non-prescription, or herbal.

7. Self-condition dreams

- They tell you where you stand with God. For example, problem areas that need addressing, those we are aware of, and those we are not aware of.

8. Courage dreams

- Courage dreams are to build you up or to strengthen your faith.

    See the example of Jacob in Genesis 31. He received a dream to choose the spotted and speckled animals; God would bless him if he did so. He needed the courage to do this because it went against his theology and understanding of animal husbandry. People of his day thought that the spotted and speckled were considered mutants, undesirable, and impure.

9. Correction dreams

- These dreams deal with attitudes and opinions.
- Do you believe your opinions can be changed in a dream or vision? Read Acts 10 and see how Peter's mind was changed.

10. Direction dreams

- Joseph was told to go home a different way than he had planned to save baby Jesus from being killed by Herod (Matthew 2:13).

11. Intercessory dreams

- They are given to cause us to pray for someone else or some situation.
- It may be for immediate results or the distant future. If you wake with a deep sense of urgency, this means it's for the current moment.

12. Prophecy and revelation dreams

- They reveal things to come.

13. Word of knowledge dreams

- They bring solutions and answers to problems and issues in our life.

- They can also relate to personal, interpersonal, job, or ministry matters.

14. Invention dreams

- These are creativity released in dreams. Many people have received a dream about a new invention, which made them a lot of money. I believe God also answers people who have prayed for His guidance in a project. Other times God entrusts new inventions to people who will advance man's life here on earth.

15. Soul dreams

- These are our desires manifested in a dream. It is an expression of our soul, mind, will, and emotions.

16. False dreams

- These dreams are full of accusations, or the enemy is provoking someone to mislead them.
- They can be a lie to get you to do something that is not in God's will.
- They come through our soul, mind, or emotions and often work through hidden pride.
- They also reveal the plans of the enemy. We then can stand against these plans and declare God's will to be done instead.

17. Dark dreams

- God allows us to see what the enemy is doing or planning.
- These dreams are usually devoid of colour. They are black and white or in a muted greyscale. In God exists all colour and light, but in the darkness, there is no colour.
- They come from the enemy revealing what he plans to do.

18. Spiritual warfare dreams

- These are warning dreams which make us aware of the attacks of the enemy against us or others.
- They will usually involve some urgent life or death issue. Your life may be in peril.
- The setting of these dreams is usually at night or in limited light.

    We can do a spiritual battle in a dream. It's called lucid dreaming. A lucid dream is defined as a dream during which dreamers are aware they are dreaming. Dreams are mentioned frequently in the Bible, and God can and does use them to speak to people. Lucid dreaming simply means being able to control your dreams. There is nothing essentially wrong with this, but it should be avoided if it becomes too much of a focus or an obsession. For Christians, being fascinated by the concept of lucid dreaming is of little or no spiritual value and might lead to an unhealthy interest in other extra-sensory phenomena. While many things are permissible for Christians, not all are beneficial (1 Corinthians 6:12).

19. Fear dreams

- Our fears come through our dreams. What we fear will show up in our dreams (Job 3:25). These are often called nightmares.
- Fear is an open door to the enemy. What we fear, we empower. What we focus on, we make room for.

20. Deliverance dreams

- These dreams remove demonic and spiritual attacks from our lives.
- We may refer to it as being delivered in a dream.

Understanding the Many Faces of God in our Dreams

God's character and personality are multifaceted. It's important to understand that the Lord will appear to us in unique ways to reveal aspects of His being. If we do not understand this, we'll often miss divine encounters with Him in our dreams. He comes to us in our dreams, and we may not realise it.

Ways God the Father Can Appear to us in our Dreams:

- As our earthly father.
- As a rich man.
- Governer, King, or Ruler.
- Spiritual Father or Leader.
- Protective figures like a Policeman, Army Sergeant, Commander.

Ways Jesus Can Appear to us in our Dreams:

- Bridegroom.
- Husband.
- Lover.
- Friend.
- Judge.
- Lion.
- Warrior.
- Shepherd.
- Fisherman.
- Carpenter.
- Teacher.

- Older brother.
- Preacher or Pastor.
- Doctor or nurse.
- Friendly dog, that's loyal and known as man's best friend.
- A natural ruler such as a Governer, King, Prime Minister.
- As a saviour or rescuer to bring you to safety.

Ways the Holy Spirit Can Appear to us in our Dreams:
- A dove.
- Giver of gifts.
- Coach or mentor.
- A wise or older man/woman.
- Wind, wine, water, fire, oil, light.
- Helper, comforter, or someone bringing peace.
- As a counsellor, that is giving you advice and counsel.
- A guide, which is a person showing you the way.
- As a faceless man or woman with a fair countenance, grey hair, dressed in light colours.

Some of the Most Common Symbols in Dreams

Following are some symbols and their possible meanings from the most common dreams that people have.

1. Dreams of Various Transportation

These include different cars, aeroplane, helicopter, bus, truck, boat, ship, tractor, motorcycle, bicycle, hot air balloon, golf cart, etc. They may represent the calling you have on your life or a type of ministry - the type of vehicle that will carry you from one point to another. Note the colour of the vehicle in your dream. If it is a car, what's the make and model? Observe who is driving it. Are you driving, or is someone else driving? If someone else is driving, who is it? Do you know the person? Is it a person from your past? If the driver is faceless, this may refer to a person who will appear sometime in your future or that the Holy Spirit Himself is your driving guide.

2. Dreams of a House

A house typically represents your life and the circumstances taking place in the house. It reflects the specific activities in your life and may even represent the church. Individual rooms of the house may mean particular things. For example, The bedroom may have something to do with issues of intimacy. Intimacy with your spouse or intimacy with God. The bathroom may represent a need for cleansing spiritually. The family room may be a clue that God wants to work on family relationships.

3. Dreams that Focuses on Names and Places

Often, the Lord speaks to us through the meaning of the names of the people, cities, and places. For example, Ellen means 'light', Elizabeth means 'My God is abundance', John means 'YAHWEH has been gracious', David means 'beloved'. If the name is a derivation, you must go to the original. For example, the following names derive from Elizabeth: Beth, Betty, Eli, Elisabeth, Elise, Eliza, Elsa, Isabella, Liza, Lisbeth. Lisa, Liz, Lizzie, Lizzy, etc.

4. Dreams of Jesus

Dreaming of Jesus may foretell that your greatest desires and goals will be realised. Seeing Jesus means to console yourself against adversity and trouble. You'll ride above a challenging situation or circumstance victoriously. The dream speaks to you and tells you that you'll be blessed with peace, joy, or contentment. Other times Jesus takes us in the Spirit to reveal the future to us or assures us of His love.

5. Dreams of Taking a Shower or Bathing

These are usually good dreams. They are cleansing dreams, revealing that things are in the process of being flushed out of your life or cleansed. They include showers, bathtubs, toilets, etc. Enjoy the showers of God's love and mercy of getting cleansed from the wrong ways of this world. Speak the blood of Jesus Christ over yourself, and get ready for a new day!

6. Dreams Concerning Storms

Storm dreams tend to represent intercessory or spiritual warfare. They are particularly common for people who have a calling or gift in the discerning of spirits. These dreams often hint negative things are coming. What kind of storm is it? Are there tornadoes involved? What colour is the storm? Tornadoes can also indicate that a change is coming, which can be good or bad but can also indicate great destruction. Dark and damaging storms foretell demonic attacks and require urgent prayer, intercession, and spiritual warfare. If it is a good storm that is not destructive, it may represent a blessing coming your way.

7. Dreams of Going to School

These dreams often centre on taking tests and may point to promotion. You might find yourself searching for your next class, which is an indication that guidance is needed. Attending a graduation ceremony may mean you have passed a test. Repeating a class may mean that you have an opportunity to learn from past failures. High School dreams can also signify that you are enrolled in the School of the Holy Spirit (H.S. = High School = Holy Spirit). These are just a few examples, but there are limitless possibilities.

Interestingly enough, the teacher is usually silent when giving a test! A teacher, on the other hand, can be a representation of Jesus. If the teacher is older with grey hair, that represents wisdom, and depending on what the teacher does in the dream; it can be a picture of the Holy Spirit coaching or mentoring you.

Dreaming you are in a school can also signify inadequacies and insecurities that have never been resolved. It can also refer to anxiety about underperformance. You may dwell on some unresolved childhood issues. It may also mean looking forward to the future instead of looking at the past.

8. Dreams of Flying or Soaring

When awakening from a dream, were you flying or soaring? You often wake up feeling exhilarated. Flying dreams deal with your spiritual capacity to rise above problems and difficulties. Ascending dreams are more unusual yet are edifying. Remember, we are seated with Christ Jesus in heavenly places far above all principalities and powers (Ephesians 2:6).

9. Dreams of Falling

What substance you fall into in the dream is a primary key to proper understanding. Dreams where you are falling may reveal a fear of losing control over some area of your life. On the positive side, you may become free from directing your own life. The primary emotions in these dreams will indicate which way to interpret them. Falling can be fearful, but it can also represent falling into the ocean of God's love.

10. Dreams of Going Through Doors

Doors represent new ways, new opportunities, new beginnings, and new advancements. It can mean God is giving you a new gift or blessing. Elevators and escalators indicate rising higher into your purpose and calling.

11. Dreams of Chasing and Being Chased

These dreams often reveal that enemies are coming against your life and purpose. On the other hand, they may indicate our passionate pursuit of God and our moving closer to Him. Ask yourself: Are you being chased? By whom? What emotions did you feel? Were you afraid of being caught? Or are you the one doing the chasing? Who are you chasing? Why? Again, what emotions did you feel during the chase? The answers to these questions and particularly the dominant emotions in the dream will often determine its interpretation. Aggressive dogs or animals chasing you means there is a demonic attack against you.

12. Dreams of Clocks and Watches

Clocks or watches in a dream reveal what time it is in your life and can be a wake-up call for the Body of Christ or a nation. It is time to be alert and watchful. These dreams may point to a Scripture verse, giving a more profound message, e.g. Are you a watchman on the wall? (Isaiah 62:6, Ezekiel 33:6).

13. Dreams with Scripture Verses

Sometimes you may have a dream in which Scriptures appear, indicating a message from God. They may be verbal quotes where you hear a voice quoting a passage, digital clock-type readouts, and dramatizations of a scene from the Bible. These dreams are often filled with wisdom.

14. Dreams of Birth

These dreams are usually not about an actual childbirth but rather about a new purpose and destiny coming into your life. There are exceptions to this when a confirmed pregnancy and birth occur. Pay attention when a name is given to the child because that usually indicates that a new season of God's purposes is birthed.

15. Dreams of Dying

Dreaming you are dying may mean transformation or a new beginning. These dreams are generally not about the actual person seen in the dream. They are usually symbolic or something that is passing away or departing from their life. It's essential to take note of the type of death and the emotion in the dream. If you wake up anxious and under pressure, pray for the person. It may be that God is warning you that someone is in trouble and may die if you do not intercede for them.

There are many testimonies of people who dreamt of a family member dying. When they woke up, they were very distressed and started praying for them. The next day the news came that their relative was in a car accident but escaped unharmed or had to be taken to the hospital with a sudden deathly illness and survived. Therefore it is vital to urgently pray since God has trusted you with the message of the danger in their life.

16. Dreams of Drowning

You are feeling overwhelmed by emotions. If you drown in the dream, it may mean a rebirth. If you survived, the drowning could indicate a relationship or situation will endure. Drowning can also signify that you are getting too deeply involved in something. Alternatively, it can mean a sense of loss of identity.

17. Dreams of Past Relationships

Seeing a person from your past does not always mean that you will renew your old relationship with that individual. Look more at what that person represented to you. A person who was a bad influence in your life may mean God is warning you not to relapse into old habits and mindsets that were not fruitful. On the other hand, a person who was a good influence in your life may represent God's desire or intention to restore good times that you thought were gone. This kind of dream may also indicate that you are tempted to fall back into old patterns or ways of thinking. Depending upon who the person is in the dream and what this person represents to you, these dreams might also indicate your need to renew your former desires and Godly passions for the good things in life.

18. Dreams of Relatives, Alive and Dead

These dreams may indicate generational issues at work, either blessings or curses or both. You need discernment as to whether to accept the blessing or cut off the curse. This is particularly true if grandparents appear in your dreams, as they will typically indicate generational issues. Seeing a deceased person or family member in your dream can also mean you are missing them or feeling regret and guilt towards them. Consider your relationship with that person. Maybe they gave you comfort or peace in a situation.

19. Dreams of Your Teeth

Dreaming of your teeth may reveal the need for wisdom. What is the condition of your teeth? Are they rotten, falling out, or are they bright and shiny? Do you have a good bite? Are you able to chew your food? Teeth represent wisdom, and often teeth appear loose in a dream. It may mean that you need understanding for something you are about to take on. The fear of the Lord is the beginning of wisdom (Proverbs 9:10). Teeth that are falling out may represent an experience of loss or the inability to understand or discern something.

20. Dreams of Being Naked or Exposed

These dreams indicate that you are becoming transparent and vulnerable. They often appear during times of transition where you move from one area in your life to the next. Depending on your particular situation, this may be exhilarating or fearful and could reveal feelings of shame. Naked dreams are not meant to produce embarrassment but rather draw you into greater intimacy with the Lord and indicate places where greater transparency is required.

21. Dreams Called Nightmares

Nightmares tend to be more frequent with children and new believers in Christ. They may reveal generational enemies and curses that need to be broken. Break the hold of the enemies of fear. Call forth the opposite presence of the love of God, which casts out fear because fear has torment (1 John 4:18).

22. Dreams of Snakes, Spiders, Bears, and Alligators

Dreaming of a snake is probably one of the most common of all animal dreams. They reveal the serpent, the devil, with his demonic hosts at work through accusation, lying, attacks, etc. Other common dreams of this nature are of spiders, bears, and even alligators. Dreams of spiders and bears reveal fear. In particular, the spider releasing its deadly poison can be a symbol of witchcraft and the occult.

23. Dreams of Dogs

After snakes, the most common animal to appear in dreams is the dog. They usually indicate friendship, loyalty, protection, and good feelings. On the other hand, dogs that are growling, attacking, biting, and chasing reveals demonic forces coming against you. Sometimes these dreams may also mean a person is about to betray you.

24. Dreams of Gemstones and Jewellery

Before man was created, God made jewellery of outstanding beauty with gold and precious stones. He made Satan a fabulous garment of jewellery before his rebellion (Ezekiel 28:13). Jewels are consecrated elements that existed before the universe and will be a part of heaven when the earth, as we know it, is no more. In Biblical times the high priest would go into God's presence with a breastplate of twelve shining jewels, and God would reveal His will to the high priest. There was one for each of the names of the sons of Israel. Each engraved like a seal for one of the twelve tribes.

There were four rows of precious stones, placed three in a row: In the first row, there were a ruby, a topaz, and beryl. In the second row were a turquoise, a sapphire, and an emerald. In the third row were a jacinth, an agate, and an amethyst, and in the fourth row, a chrysolite, an onyx, and a jasper (Exodus 28:17-21). Jewels have always been a sign of favour. They are universal symbols of beauty and wealth. God considers His people His jewels, and His goal is to beautify them that they might shine like jewels and be as durable as jewels. The prophet Zechariah describes the day of God's coming to rescue His people in Zechariah 9:16-17, *"The Lord their God will save them on that day as the flock of His people. They will sparkle in His land like jewels in a crown. How attractive and beautiful they will be!"* The foundations and city walls of the New Jerusalem that will come down from heaven after the millennial reign of Jesus on earth will be decorated with every kind of precious stone (Revelation 21:19-20).

Understanding God's Messages

Many of our dreams will be insignificant, but when we obey all the small messages from God in our daily walk, we'll be ready when the important instructions come. In an interview with Larry King, the well-known evangelist Billy Graham was asked, *"It must be rewarding for you to look back on your life and not have to live with regrets."* Billy Graham answered Larry, *"I am the greatest failure of all men. I was too much with men and too little with God. I was too busy with business meetings and even conducting services. I should have been more with God, and people would've sensed God's presence about me when they were with me."* Let this be a lesson for us from Billy Graham, who is now with the Lord. Let's make more time for God in our daily life and not keep ourselves busy with all the different works for God!

During Jesus' earthly ministry recorded in the four gospels, he often talked in parables. Matthew 13:34-35 says, *"Jesus spoke all these things to the crowd in parables; he did not say anything to them without using a parable. So was fulfilled what was spoken through the prophet: I will open my mouth in parables, I will utter things hidden since the creation of the world."*

To get familiar with Jesus' metaphoric way of storytelling, study the New Testament books: Matthew, Mark, Luke, and John. It will help you understand His symbolic dream language to you. Here is an example of a possible dream: You dream that you are walking with a group of people and a Senior Tour Guide, then you get distracted by something. You tell them to go ahead, and you will catch up later. By the time you try to get back to them, you have to go through pools of water. You wonder how they managed to stay dry while you get wet. In this dream, the tour guide could represent Jesus because He can walk on water (Matthew 14:25-27). The group who stayed with Him could also walk on water, just as Peter in the above mentioned Scripture. You left them for a short while, and when you tried to get back to the group, you got wet.

What do we learn from this example? When we stay with Jesus, our life journey will be easier than going by ourselves. We want to stay with Jesus to keep dry and not miss out on the miracles while moving with Him.

At the back of this book are more dream symbols and possible meanings. I hope this dream interpretation section makes you excited to hear what God wants to speak to you. Do not forget to ask the Holy Spirit to help you interpret God's divine messages! Following are two of my dreams as exercise.

Two of My Dreams as Exercise

DREAM 1	Title: Huge Artificial Intelligence Bees instructed not to hurt me
Date	October 2019
Emotion	I felt at peace and amazed
Circumstances	My life was peaceful
Dream Description	A man is going to take care of me and give me food. As we walked into a garden with many fruit trees, he said, wait a bit, and he walked over to a tree. Hand-size bees dropped down from the inside of the tree to listen to what the man is saying. I thought he was speaking to the bee creatures that they must not harm me. Their colouring looked like bees which are yellow and black, and they had wings and stingers. There were also other small animals, like zebras, that were also yellow and black with wings and stingers. They were flying like bees. I got the feeling that they were operating as spies. I heard them saying to the man, 'Let us look at her to recognise her in the future'. They came over to me and flew up and down, looking at me with their big eyes.
Possible Meaning	The man in the dream is Jesus, who will take care of me and feed me. The bees and animal creatures were evil spirits. Jesus went over to talk to them. He commanded them not to hurt me.

Dream 2	Title: A man that I knew was pregnant and has gone into labour
Date	November 2019
Emotion	Expectation
Circumstances	Praying and waiting for God's response
Dream Description	I dreamt about a pregnant male friend who was going into labour at home while his wife was at work. The doctor and nurses came out to the house to help him give birth. His daughters were also there to help. The doctor said to them, they never had a case like that in Australia, and they see it as a first in the study towards men being pregnant and in labour. The man gave birth to a baby boy, and when his wife got home, the baby was still in the incubator. One of their daughters gave her mother a quick update on how it all went and that it is a baby boy. She made herself a coffee to be ready for when the doctors come back.
Possible Meaning	Giving birth represents the beginning of a new adventure, new idea, project, or ministry. A man giving birth means it is supernatural because men cannot be pregnant. The doctor said that this has never happened before and is a first. This new beginning of something will take longer to develop because the baby is in the incubator. The doctor may represent Jesus, and the nurses, angels. God has planted a vision or new idea in the man. He has called the man to incubate it or meditate on it until it is fully developed and ready for the world.

CHAPTER 6

THE RAPTURE, TRIBULATION, AND THE RETURN OF CHRIST

For years I went to church listening to preachers and many different sermons on television, the internet, and CDs. I learned who Jesus Christ is and what He accomplished for us through His crucifixion. He was resurrected by God's Dunamis *(the miracle power, strength, and force of God)* three days after His burial. For forty days after that, He appeared and communicated with hundreds of people on earth who bore witness to Him being resurrected (1 Corinthians 15:3-9). After this, He ascended into heaven to sit on the right hand of God the Father, sending us the wonderful gift of His Spirit to be with us every day. What an incredible privilege that we as followers of Christ have had over the past two thousand years and still have today, where God's Spirit is in our hearts connecting us to Jesus and the Father. This remarkable story did not end there!

Jesus Christ promised us that He will return to earth! But before He returns for good to take up His place as King and Ruler over the whole world, He promised to extract His bride *(The Church / Born again believers)* from a troubled and chaotic earth. Believers know it as the *Rapture*, which is described in 1 Thessalonians 4:16-17 as being 'caught up' in the air, *"For the Lord himself will descend from heaven with a cry of command, with the voice of an archangel, and with the sound of the trumpet of God. And the dead in Christ will rise first. Then we who are alive, who are left, will be <u>caught up</u> together with them in the clouds to meet the Lord in the air, and so we will always be with the Lord."*

The Rapture

From the above Scripture, we understand that Jesus will descend from heaven with a loud sound announcing the rapture. Some Bible scholars believe that only born again believers, who have the seal of the Holy Spirit, will hear the trumpet sound of God announcing the rapture. The unbelievers and unsaved humanity may only hear the sound of a thunderstorm, not knowing what is happening, until they realise that their friends and family members who were followers of Jesus Christ have disappeared from the earth.

The Rapture signifies the bodily resurrection of the dead in Christ and the bodily transformation of those born again Christians still alive. It will be an instantaneous change for those who are alive when Christ returns, as explained in 1 Corinthians 15:52-53, *"In a moment, in the twinkling of an eye, at the last trumpet. For the trumpet will sound, and the dead will be raised incorruptible, and we shall be changed. For this corruptible must put on incorruption, and this mortal must put on immortality."* Jesus' feet will not even touch the earth when He meets all saved humanity in the clouds. The purpose of the Rapture is that Jesus plans to protect His Church *(bride/body)* from the extreme suffering that will come upon the earth during the seven years of tribulation.

After Jesus meets the saints or His elect in the air, they will all go with Him to heaven for the marriage of the Lamb (Revelation 19:7). In Revelation 19:9, we read, *"Blessed are those who are called to the marriage supper of the Lamb! (Jesus)"* The celebration between Jesus and the Church is compared to a marriage celebration and will run for seven earthly years. Heaven's time clock is not the same as our earthly clock, and the seven years on earth maybe only seven days in heaven. I say this because Jesus was born of a Jewish mother and raised in the Jewish community and culture. According to Ancient Jewish tradition, a marriage celebration ran over seven days.

To understand the marriage supper of the Lamb, which is the occasion that the Christian Church on earth is looking forward to, we have to look at the wedding customs when Jesus was here in the flesh. These customs are still in practice today!

The three parts of a Jewish wedding consisted of the following:

1. A Marriage Contract. The contract was signed by the parents of the bride and bridegroom. The bridegroom would also sign the contract and agree to pay a dowry *(down payment)* to the bride or her parents. The signed contract was given to the bride-to-be, and when she was happy with the content, she would also sign it. This step started the betrothal period that we call engagement. The bridegroom would then go away to prepare a house for his bride, usually an extension to his father's house. Normally it would be for two years of preparation without seeing his bride.

2. A Torchlight Parade Through the Streets. When the house is ready for his bride, and the bridegroom's father had approved the house, he will fetch his bride. Accompanied by his male friends, the bridegroom will go to the bride's house at midnight, thereby creating a torchlight parade with oil lamps through the streets. It would not have been a surprise to the bride when the bridegroom was coming to get her, for she knew well in advance when the event would take place, and she would be ready with her maidens.

3. The Marriage Supper. During the time of Jesus, a marriage supper would go on for days like the wedding in Cana described in John 2:1-11. The marriage supper of the Lamb, as described in Revelation 19:7-9, is the third phase of the wedding feast. John, who wrote the book of Revelation, did not skip the first two phases of the wedding custom but communicated that they had already happened. The first phase was completed on earth when each Christian placed their faith in Jesus Christ. In this case, the bridegroom's parent *(God the Father)* paid the dowry, which was the blood of His Son, Jesus Christ, shed on His bride's behalf. The Church *(true ekklesia)* is therefore betrothed to Christ. Born again Christians live in the third phase today, where we are awaiting our Bridegroom's return, to come and rapture us to go to the marriage supper in heaven.

Prophets and scholars studying the Bible reckon that the rapture of the church can be at any moment because most prophecies that must have happened before the rapture already did. Therefore, we have to live our lives as if Jesus is coming today. Be ready as the Bible teaches us and be expectant.

According to the Scripture, many who say they are Christians will miss being caught up in the Rapture because they did not have a personal relationship with our Lord Jesus Christ (Matthew 7:21-23).

The Tribulation

As soon as the Church of Christ gets raptured, the seven-year tribulation will begin. While the wedding celebration in heaven is taking place, the world will go through extreme suffering. The ancient prophet Jeremiah called it "the time of Jacob's trouble" (Jeremiah 30:7). Evil will flourish on the earth, and God's wrath will be revealed toward the wicked. He will leave them to destroy each other. Two-thirds of the earth's population will be destroyed by wars, persecutions, famines, and pestilences. In Zechariah 13:8, we read, *"In the whole land, declares the LORD, two thirds shall be cut off and perish, and one third shall be left alive."*

The tribulation period is divided into two phases, according to the Book of Revelation. During the first half *(three and a half years)*, it will look like everything goes on as usual. The last half *(three and a half years)* of the tribulation is called the 'Great Tribulation'. At the start of the seven-year tribulation, a man known as the Antichrist will come into power.

He will win the Jews over when he rebuilds their temple. By bringing peace and doing signs and wonders, he will mislead them into thinking he is the Messiah or Christ who will save the world (Daniel chapters 9-11). At first, it will look like he successfully restored peace on earth, but suddenly all hell will break loose. Around the midpoint of these seven years, there will be some sort of assassination attempt on his life, which he will miraculously survive. It is then when Satan will possess this ruler. It will become impossible to be a follower of Christ then. Jesus said in Matthew 24:21, *"For then there will be great tribulation, such as has not been since the beginning of the world until this time, no, nor ever shall be."*

People will go through enormous persecution. Weird things will happen and implemented to control the population. During these seven years, the Antichrist and his followers will implement the Mark of the Beast. After three and a half years since the tribulation started, the Antichrist will commit the abomination of desolation, which means he will erect an image of himself in the temple of the Jews and command people to worship him (2 Thessalonians 2:4). When the Jews see this abomination of desolation, they will flee into the mountains, and it will mark the second half of the tribulation, called the Great Tribulation.

The worldwide vaccination program recently implemented for COVID-19 is a forerunner for the Mark of the Beast. It makes people used to the new way of living for when the Antichrist will come into power. According to many health practitioners worldwide, the COVID-19 vaccine is not genuine as we know it because it took many years to decades to develop previous vaccines. One of the leading scientists in vaccine creating, Dr Geert Vanden Bossche, PhD DVM, explained that the COVID-19 vaccines work to break down the natural antibodies in the human body. That means the body's natural defence mechanism will no longer perform as God created it, and man will fall ill quicker and eventually die sooner. The effects of these vaccines are irreversible once injected. It seems like it works similarly to HIV *(human immunodeficiency virus)*, where the virus attacks the body's immune system. If HIV is not treated, it can lead to AIDS *(acquired immunodeficiency syndrome)*. There is currently no effective cure. Once people get HIV, they have it for life.

I understood that people who received the COVID-19 vaccine would no longer have a normal healthy life. Some people already died within twenty-four hours, and others can die in a few weeks, especially those whose immune system is compromised. In comparison, some people may take a few years of suffering different illnesses because their body's immune system is not that strong anymore, to where the body eventually gives in and perish. Research Dr Geert Vanden Bossche to see in detail the after-effects of the COVID-19 vaccines. I have listened to Del Bigtree from *The High Wire* explaining the interview between Dr Phillip McMillan and Dr Geert Vanden Bossche, called 'Vaccine Disaster Ahead'. That was an eye-opener and a must-see! You can also search the interview on Youtube: *Mass Vaccination in a Pandemic – Benefits versus Risks: Interview with Geert Vanden Bossche*. Hopefully, it is still available on Youtube by the time you read this! Pastor John Hagee called COVID-19, "The dress rehearsal for the New World Order!"

It brings us again to the fact that Satan wants to kill and destroy mankind at all costs. I want to come back to the prophecy regarding the 'Mark of the Beast'. According to Bible prophecy, it will be imprinted in a person's right hand or on their forehead. No one will be able to buy or sell without the mark, that is, the name of the beast or the number of his name, which is 666. Revelation 13:16-18 says, *"It also forced all people, great and small, rich and poor, free and slave, to receive a mark on their right hands or their foreheads, so that they could not buy or sell unless they had the mark, which is the name of the beast or the number of its name. This calls for wisdom. Let the person who has insight calculate the number of the beast, for it is the number of a man. That number is 666."*

The Antichrist and His followers will control humankind with the mark so that they will lose their identity. It will not just be a mark but a pledge of allegiance! A sign of devotion to the Antichrist *(Satan himself)*, denying Jesus Christ as the Messiah! The people who will accept the Mark of the Beast of the Antichrist will stand no chance of reuniting with Jesus Christ. They will lose their salvation forever. There will be no turning back from that.

Stories appeared in the media about technology that will allow the Antichrist or Evil Human Dictator to number and track every person on earth. Many people believe it will be a techno tattoo or a technological device like a microchip implanted underneath the skin. This technology already exists today, and many people have already received this chip!

The microchip or RFID *(radio-frequency identification)* is an advanced identification process wherein an item or individual is tagged with an identification number. A computerized reader can access any stored information by scanning the unique serial number of a tag using radio waves. The tagged object needs to be only within a few feet of a reader to process an identification number, which is more advanced than today's barcode technology. The microchip is the size of a grain of rice, and the procedure of inserting it through the skin does not take more than ten minutes. Since the microchip was created in 1958, it went through advancements and is used today in phones, swipe cards, merchandise, and vehicles.

In 1998, Professor of Cybernetics, Kevin Warwick, had a chip implanted in his hand. It is a way of exploring the transhumanist idea that merging technology with the human body, which is the next step in humanity's evolution. The term *cybernetics* comes from the ancient Greek word *kybernetikos (meaning good at steering)*, referring to the helmsman's art, e.g., control. In the first half of the 19th century, the French physicist André-Marie Ampère, in his classification of the science, suggested that the still non-existent science of governments' control be called cybernetics. The Collins dictionary defines the term 'cybernetics' as 'the science which involves studying the way electronic machines and human brains work, and developing machines that do things or think like people'.

In 2015 in Sweden, a high-tech office block started offering employees the option of getting a tiny and miniature sensor beneath their skin as a substitute for the swipe card to pay for food at the café or access amenities such as printers. At the same time, a remote-control contraceptive chip was created by Massachusetts-based MicroCHIPS. This chip allowed women to turn shots of birth control medicine on and off.

Digital RFID tattoos are also obtainable for those who want to monitor their body by measuring temperature, UV exposure, hydration levels, and other bodily factors. Microchip technology is also used in hospitals to diagnose and treat patients.

Despite the numerous claimed benefits, Microchip technology causes concern for many over improper handling of sensitive data and privacy violations. It is clear that if someone can read it, there is always someone smart enough to hack it. Many evangelical Christians and prophecy watchers are convinced that the RFID chip inserted into the human body is the prophesied Mark of the Beast.

Executives of *Three Square Market* said the microchip is not a GPS and is not used to monitor an individual's day-to-day activities. For instance, at *Three Square Market*, the microchip does not monitor an employee's bathroom breaks or lunch hours. However, the possibilities are endless. The microchip can be encoded with medical records, making it easier to determine the need for a booster shot for tetanus or health care access. Microchips have already been implanted in pets. The *Transportation Security Administration* (TSA) could use microchips to execute screening passengers for air travel speedily. In contrast, countries worldwide could use it for multiple purposes, such as collecting fares. Microchip technology could also be used for identifying travellers with fake IDs.

Many people disagree that RFID or microchip technology is the 'Mark of the Beast' as prophesied in the Bible. However, the origins of these facts do raise serious questions regarding the merging of computers with human bodies. Although some will say it is pure speculation, we need to be aware that it does not matter the so-called benefits of a microchip, digital tattoo, or vaccine. We must be very cautious not to have anything injected into our bodies, implanted underneath our skin, on the forehead, or the right hand as God warns us in Revelation 13:16-17. We always have to keep in mind that our body is the temple of the Holy Spirit!

The Antichrist will be the worst dictator that the world has ever seen. He will oppose Christ and the Christian Church and is coming to kill the Jews and the followers of Christ. He wants to worship Satan and take the place of Jesus Christ, claiming to be God (2 Thessalonians 2:3-4). Revelation 12 describes how the dragon *(Satan)* gives power to the beast *(Antichrist)*.

People who missed the Rapture and thereby living through the tribulation period, not accepting the Mark of the Beast, will get another chance to be saved and live with Jesus in heaven for all of eternity. However, they will pay with their lives and their blood (Revelation 20). It will be very tough to keep following Jesus to survive on earth during this time. Those who deny the Antichrist will be beheaded. The apostle John received the revelation and visions of the end time from Jesus Christ. In Revelation 20:4, he describes it as follows, *"And I saw thrones, and they sat upon them, and judgment was given unto them: and I saw the souls of them that were beheaded for the witness of Jesus, and for the Word of God, and which had not worshipped the beast, neither his image, neither had received his mark upon their foreheads or in their hands; and they lived and reigned with Christ a thousand years."*

Another entity will be working with the Antichrist during the tribulation called the false prophet (Revelation 13:11-15, Revelation 16:13, Revelation 19:20, Revelation 20:10). He is going to attempt and organise peace amongst all religions by creating a One World Religion. Meaning all religions are praying to the same God. If a person is genuinely spiritual, they will find their way to Jesus Christ as the Bible teaches us and not trying to unite all the religions by creating one god to fit all! I've discussed in chapter 3 the reasons why all religions can't worship the same god.

On the 5th of February 2016, ISKCON News put a video online of Michael Snyder reporting that Pope Francis very clearly expressed his belief that the major religions are different paths to the same 'god'. He also said that while people from various global faiths may be "seeking God or meeting God in different ways", it is important to keep in mind that "we are all children of God". Through these statements, the Pope completely abandoned any notion that a relationship with God is only available through Jesus Christ. As he has done throughout his papacy, he continues to lead the groundwork for the coming One World Religion that will fit in nicely with the One World Order and Antichrist.

At the time the apostle John received the vision of the end times in heaven, one of the elders asked him in Revelation 7:13, *"These in white robes, who are they, and where did they come from?"* John answered him, *"Sir, you know."* The elder then said in Revelation 7:14-15, *"These are they who have <u>come out of the great tribulation</u>; they have washed their robes and made them white in the blood of the Lamb; therefore, they are before the throne of God and serve him day and night in his temple; and he who sits on the throne will shelter them with his presence."* It will be those who were brutally killed and beheaded for their faith in Christ.

I have recently listened to a remarkable American Evangelist, Robert Breaker, on YouTube, who gave the following teaching: From Moses's time, till the crucifixion of Jesus, the people on the earth were falling under the 'Law'. In ancient times people were judged by God according to the Ten Commandments and its bylaws. Therefore, people had to work hard not to partake in these sins. There were six hundred and thirteen other commandments of Moses, which they also had to follow, called the Mitzvot. After Jesus's crucifixion, God's judgement has turned to 'grace and mercy'. He gave His only begotten Son to die on the cross for all the sins of mankind, and through the blood of Jesus, we are saved. The current time that we are living in is called the 'Church Age'. Jesus has done everything for us to forgive our sins and to save us from eternal damnation. We do not have to do any works ourselves, apart from accepting God's only begotten Son and His finished work on the cross. In Revelation 20:4, when John saw thrones in heaven for those who had been beheaded for their testimony in Jesus, it means they will die for Jesus to make it to heaven. It is clear that 'grace and mercy' will not help people during the tribulation period anymore.

Of course, people who have accepted Jesus today are not perfect and are still redeemed sinners. But through Jesus, we are made righteous before God, as I have already discussed in this book. The Bible has many beautiful Scriptures on how we were made righteous. Here are three: 2 Corinthians 5:21, *"For He hath made Him to be sin for us, who knew no sin; that we might be made the righteousness of God in Him."* Romans 10:4, *"For Christ is the end of the law for righteousness to everyone who believes."* Romans 3:21-22, *"But now apart from the law the righteousness of God has been made known, to which the Law and the Prophets* testify. This righteousness is given through faith in Jesus Christ to all who believe. There is no difference between Jew and Gentile."

By the time the saved church *(body of Christ)* is raptured, the Holy Spirit will also depart from the earth because He lives in every born-again believer. Up to the time of the rapture, the Holy Spirit will be the restraining force in the world to limited Satan's devastating work. Without the Holy Spirit, evil will rule the world during the tribulation period like never before!

The Return of Jesus Christ

Christ's return is known as the *Second Coming*. There are over fifteen hundred Old Testament passages of Scripture that refer to the *Second Coming* of Christ. There are three hundred and thirty verses of Scripture in the New Testament, or about one out of every twenty-five verses, that directly refer to the *Second Coming*. Jesus himself refers to His *Second Coming* twenty-one times, and over fifty times, we are encouraged to be ready for His return. This *Second Coming* is a central theme throughout the Old and New Testaments. Only the subject of faith is mentioned more times in the Bible than the *Second Coming* of Christ. Every time the first coming of Jesus Christ is mentioned in the Bible, the *Second Coming* is mentioned eight times. Jesus said, *"For the Son of Man is going to come in His Father's glory with His angels, and then He will reward each person according to what he has done"* - (Matthew 16:27).

At the end of the marriage celebration in heaven between Jesus and His bride *(The Church)*, and the end of the seven-year tribulation on earth, Jesus will return with His army of angels and saints. The final sign of Jesus's *Second Coming* will be when a massive worldly army with millions of soldiers are marching up to Jerusalem to destroy His beloved city, Jerusalem, and the Jewish people. According to Scripture, it's called the 'Battle of Armageddon' and will take place in the valley of Jezreel, at the foot of the hill called Megiddo in Israel. The word Armageddon means Mount of Megiddo. This battle will be the final battle between the kings of the earth under demonic leadership and God's forces.

The world government formed at the beginning of the *Great Tribulation* is scheduled in prophecy to endure for forty-two months or three and a half years (Revelation 13:5). The world ruler will be Satan's masterpiece as a counterfeit of Christ. He is the actual supreme dictator of the entire world, and in a sense, Satan incarnated. He will undoubtedly be a brilliant man with a dynamic personality, but he will be dominated entirely or controlled by Satan.

On the last day of the great tribulation, during the battle of Armageddon, Jesus Christ will appear on a white horse. His heavenly army of angels and saints will be with Him to engage in a short but decisive battle with His enemies. John described in Revelation 19:11-16 what he saw when Jesus returns, *"I saw heaven standing open and there before me was a white horse, whose rider is called Faithful and True. With justice, He judges and wages war. His eyes are like blazing fire, and on His head are many crowns. He has a name written on Him that no one knows but he himself. He is dressed in a robe dipped in blood, and His name is the Word of God. The armies of heaven followed Him, riding on white horses and dressed in fine linen, white and clean. Coming out of His mouth is a sharp sword with which to strike down the nations. "He will rule them with an iron sceptre." He treads the winepress of the fury of the wrath of God Almighty. On His robe and His thigh, he has this name written:* **King of kings and Lord of lords.**"

The sword coming out of Jesus's mouth described here is not a literal sword, but it is a resonance sound wave weapon that will destroy the armies marching to Jerusalem. It represents the Word of God *(Bible)*. Therefore, by speaking in the authority of God, Jesus will kill the evil nations. Just as the world was spoken into existence, the evil on this earth will be destroyed through the spoken Word of God. Amen and Glory to God Almighty! In another Scripture in the Old Testament, Hosea 6:5, God said to His unrepentant nation, Israel, that He will kill them with the words of His Mouth, and His judgements will go forth like the sun.

The *Second Coming* of Jesus, described in Revelation 19, will be like lightning that will be seen from everywhere. Jesus will physically return to Jerusalem the same way as He ascended into heaven from the Mount of Olives at the end of His first coming. While the

Apostles were watching, two men in white robes stood beside them said, *"Men of Galilee, why do you stand gazing up into heaven? This same Jesus, who was taken up from you into heaven, will so come in like manner as you saw Him go into heaven"* – Acts 1:11.

Zechariah describes Jesus' *Second Coming* as follows: *"And in that day His feet will stand on the Mount of Olives, which faces Jerusalem on the east. And the Mount of Olives shall be split in two, from east to west, making a very large valley; half of the mountain shall move towards the north and half of it towards the south. Then you shall flee through My mountain valley, for the mountain valley shall reach to Azal. Yes, you shall flee as you fled from the earthquake in the days of Uzziah, king of Judah. Thus, the Lord my God will come, and all the saints with You"* (Zechariah 14:4-5).

During this historical event, when enormous earthquakes occur worldwide, the Mount of Olives will split in two. A very dramatic reconciliation will occur between the remnant of Israel and their once-rejected Messiah, Jesus Christ. The Jews who fled to the mountains during the mid-tribulation will return to the Mount of Olives to meet their Messiah. They will do so despite the great danger posed by the deployment of massive antichrist forces in and around Jerusalem and other places in the Middle East. According to the prophecies in Daniel 12, they will know that three and a half years had elapsed from the day on which the false messiah *(Antichrist)* declared himself to be God in the temple in Jerusalem, until the day on which the true Messiah will make His appearance. In Daniel 12:11, we read: *"And from the time that the daily sacrifice is taken away, and the abomination of desolation is set up, there shall be one thousand two hundred and ninety days"* Just before the Day of Atonement, which will bring this period to a close, the remaining Jews will go to the Mount of Olives unarmed, only trusting in God's intervention.

Despite their anxiety due to the Battle of Armageddon raging, they will approach Jerusalem. They will despair at a particular stage, fearing that their hope is gone and that they will be killed. At that critical moment, their Messiah *(Jesus Christ)* will come. When His feet touch the Mount of Olives, it will split in two, and the darkness of God's judgements will engulf the enemy forces. The Jews will take refuge from the Antichrist's pursuing troops in the east to west valley, formed by the splitting in two of the mountain.

On that day, the Jews will be most surprised to see that their Messiah has pierced marks in His hands, as described by Zechariah. When they see the marks of the nails in the hands of Jesus, they will ask Him, *"What are these wounds in your hands?"* Then He will answer, *"Those with which I was wounded in the house of My friends"* (Zechariah 13:6). It will be a heart-stirring moment when Israel shows great remorse for their sins, particularly the fact that their fathers rejected their Messiah during His first coming. Zechariah 12:10 says, *"They will mourn for Him as one mourns for his only son, and grieve for Him as one grieves for a firstborn."*

After this most significant event in human history, the millennial *(thousand years)* reign of Jesus Christ on the earth will begin. He will rule and reign over the people together with His saints (Revelation 20:6; Daniel 7:18, 27; Revelation 3:21; 5:10, Jeremiah 23:5, Revelation 19:7-8). They will uphold justice and righteousness in the land. It will not be a spiritual reign, but a physical reign as we experience on earth now. The difference is that our Lord Jesus Christ and His saints will have glorified bodies (Philippians 3:21, 1 John 3:2, 1 Corinthians 15:51-53). The glorified body will be far more powerful than our present "weak" earthly body. This new body will have unique abilities, such as: no longer suffering any physical sickness or death, having a spiritualised nature that will be able to pass through walls and closed doors, the ability to bilocate and travel great distances in an instant, be free from any deformity and will be clothed in beauty and radiance according to Matthew 13:43.

At the start of Jesus' millennial reign, the Antichrist and the False Prophet are the first ones to be thrown into the Lake of Fire and Brimstone (Revelation 19:20). Satan will be bound in the bottomless pit for a thousand years (Revelation 20:2). Those people who were beheaded because of their testimony in Jesus, and those who did not worship the beast or received his mark on their foreheads or hands, will also reign with Jesus for a thousand years. The second death has no power over them, and they will be priests of Father God and Christ. The rest of the dead did not come to life until the thousand years end (Revelation 20:4-5).

When the thousand years are over, Satan will be released from his prison to go out and deceive the nations in the four corners of the earth again. He will gather them together as many as the sand of the sea to battle against God's people. They will march across the world and surround God's people in the city that He loves *(Jerusalem)*. Fire will come down from heaven and devour them. The devil who deceived them will also be thrown into the lake of burning sulfur, where the beast and the false prophet are. They will be tormented day and night forever and ever (Revelation 20:7-10).

After all this, the *Great White Throne Judgement* will take place. This event will involve everyone who did not accept Jesus Christ as their Lord and Saviour during their life on earth. In the Revelation given to John of the end time, he saw this, *"I saw the dead, great and small, standing before the throne, and books were opened. Another book was opened, which is the book of life. The dead were judged according to what they had done as recorded in the books. The sea gave up the dead that was in it, and death and Hades gave up the dead that were in them, and each person was judged according to what they had done. Then death and Hades were thrown into the lake of fire. The lake of fire is the second death. Anyone whose name was not found written in the book of life was thrown into the lake of fire."* (Revelation 20:12-15)

Christians will not be present at the *Great White Throne Judgement*. They will participate in a separate judgement known as the *Judgement Seat of Christ*, which is the final test to determine their suitability for heaven (2 Corinthians 5:10). When we stand in front of the Judgement Seat of Christ, our faithful service to Him will be evaluated and rewarded.

Now that all God's enemies *(Satan, his fallen angels, unsaved humanity)* have been cast into the Lake of Fire, God will be giving the rest of saved humanity their final reward - the New Heaven and the New Earth. He who was sitting on the throne in heaven said this to John, *"I am making everything new! Write this down, for these words are trustworthy and true. It is done. I am the Alpha and the Omega, the Beginning and the End. To the thirsty, I will give water without cost from the spring of the water of life."* (Revelation 21:5-6)

The first heaven and the first earth will pass away. There will be no more sea. The Holy City (New Jerusalem) will come down from heaven, prepared as a bride beautifully dressed for her husband. God's dwelling place will be among His people. He will wipe every tear from their eyes. There will be no more death or mourning or crying or pain, for the old order of things has passed away. (Revelation 21:1-5)

There will not be a temple in the city anymore because the Lord God Almighty and the Lamb are its temple. The city does not need the sun or the moon to shine on it, for the glory of God gives it light, and the Lamb (Jesus) is its lamp. The nations will walk by its light, and the kings of the earth will bring their splendour into it. Its gates will never be shut, and there will be no night there. The glory and honour of the nations will be brought into it. Nothing impure will ever enter it, nor will anyone who does what is shameful or deceitful, but only those whose names are written in the Lamb's book of life. (Revelation 21:22-27).

Praise God Almighty! I pray that you'll be ready for Jesus Christ's Return!

Below are a few Bible verses describing and confirming the Rapture and Jesus's *Second Coming* to earth:

1 Thessalonians 4:16-18, *"For the Lord Himself will descend from heaven with a shout, with the voice of an archangel, and with the trumpet of God. And the dead in Christ will rise first. Then we who are alive and remain shall be caught up together with them in the clouds to meet the Lord in the air. And thus, we shall always be with the Lord. 18 Therefore comfort one another with these words."*

Revelation 1:7, Regarding Jesus Second Coming, we read, *"Behold, He cometh with clouds, and every eye shall see him, and they also which pierced him: and all kindreds of the earth shall wail because of Him. Even so, Amen."*

In Revelation 22:12-13, Jesus said, *"Look, I am coming soon! My reward is with me, and I will give to each person according to what they have* done. *I am the Alpha and the Omega, the First and the Last, the Beginning and the End."*

Matthew 16:27, *"For the Son of Man is going to come in his Father's glory with his angels, and then he will reward each person according to what they have done."*

Titus 2:13, *"While we wait for the blessed hope, the appearing of the glory of our great God and Saviour, Jesus Christ."*

Matthew 24:27, *"For as lightning that comes from the east is visible even in the west, so will be the coming of the Son of Man (Jesus)."*

1 Thessalonians 5:2, Apostle Paul wrote, *"For you, yourselves are fully aware that the day of the Lord will come like a thief in the night."*

Matthew 26:64, Jesus said, *"You have said so. But I tell you, from now on, you will see the Son of Man seated at the right hand of Power and coming on the clouds of heaven."*

Revelations 16:15, Jesus said, *"Behold, I am coming like a thief! Blessed is the one who stays awake, keeping his garments on, that he may not go about naked and be seen exposed!"*

The Signs of Jesus Christ's Second Coming

Jesus is coming again! Non-Christians will find it hard to believe that we live in the last days when Jesus will return, but it is all in the Bible. Two thousand years ago, Jesus said this to His disciples in John 14:2-3, *"In My Father's house are many mansions; if it were not so, I would have told you. I go to prepare a place for you. And if I go and prepare a place for you, I will come again and receive you to Myself; that where I am, there you may be also."* God is alerting believers of the soon return of His Son through what are called 'signs of the times'. By looking at the Jewish wedding customs that I've discussed earlier, this Bible verse tells us that our Bridegroom *(Jesus)* will come and get the born again Church after He completed our house.

In Matthew 24 and Luke 21, the disciples of Jesus asked Him what will signify His coming at the end of this age. Below are some signs in no particular order:

Luke 21:29-31, *"Then He (Jesus) spoke to them a parable: "Look at the fig tree and all the trees. When they are already budding, you see and know for yourselves that summer is now near. So you also, when you see these things happening, know that the Kingdom of God is near."*

1. *Men posing as Jesus will try to deceive people in the last days.*

   Jesus said in Matthew 24:5, "For many will come in my name, claiming, 'I am the Messiah,' and will deceive many." For false messiahs and false prophets will appear and perform great signs and wonders to deceive, if possible, even the elect (Matthew 24:24). If anyone tells you, 'There he is, out in the wilderness,' do not go out; or, 'Here he is, in the inner rooms,' do not believe it. For as lightning that comes from the east is visible even in the west, so will be the coming of the Son of Man (Matthew 24:26-27).

2. *You will hear of wars and rumours of wars but see to it that you are not alarmed. Such things must happen, but the end is still to come. Nation will rise against nation, and kingdom against kingdom. There will be famines and earthquakes in various places. All these are the beginning of birth pains (Matthew 24:6-8).*

3. *There will be great earthquakes, famines and pestilences in various places, and fearful events and great signs from heaven (Luke 21:11).*

4. *But before all these things, they will lay their hands on you and persecute you. You will be betrayed even by parents, brothers, relatives and friends. They will put some of you to death. You will be hated by all for My name's (Jesus Christ) sake (Luke 21:12-19).*

5. *Lawlessness will abound, and the love of many will grow cold (Matthew 24:12).*

6. *When you see the 'abomination of desolation,' spoken of by Daniel the prophet, standing in the holy place" (whoever reads, let him understand), "then let those who are in Judea flee to the mountains" (Matthew*

24:15). It is when the Antichrist declares himself God in the temple of Jerusalem.

7. *The Gospel of the Kingdom will be preached in all the world as a witness to the nations. Then the end will come! (Matthew 24:14).*

8. *There will be signs in the sun, in the moon, and the stars, and on the earth distress of nations, with perplexity, the sea and the waves roaring (Luke 21:25).*

9. *Immediately after the tribulation, the sun will be darkened, and the moon will not give its light. The stars will fall from heaven, and the powers of the heavens will be shaken. Then the sign of the Son of Man will appear in heaven, and all the tribes of the earth will mourn, and they will see the Son of Man coming on the clouds of heaven with power and great glory (Matthew 24:29).* Jesus said in Luke 21:28, *"Now when these things begin to happen, look up and lift your heads because your redemption draws near."*

10. *Therefore keep watch, because you do not know on what day your Lord will come. But understand this: If the owner of the house had known at what time of night the thief was coming, he would have kept watch and would not have let his house be broken into. So you also must be ready because the Son of Man will come at an hour when you do not expect him (Matthew 24:42-44).* Paul makes it clear in 1 Thessalonians 5:1-6 that Jesus' statement does not apply to believers: *"But you, brethren, are not in darkness, that the day should overtake you like a thief...."*

Other signs mentioned in the Book of Daniel, Zechariah and Revelation:

1. The Jews were dispersed from their land in 70 A.D. According to the Scripture, they would re-occupy Israel (Luke 21:24), the resurgence of Israeli military strength (Zechariah 12:6), and the re-focusing of world politics on Israel (Zechariah 12:3). On the 14th of May 1948, Israel officially declared an independent state with David Ben-Gurion, the Jewish

Agency head, as the prime minister. Since then, Jews have been immigrating back to their land.

2. The rise of an aggressive, Fundamentalist Islamic Power (Daniel 11:40,42-43).

3. There will be a coalition of European nations that will form a confederation centred in the old Roman empire (Daniel 2:41-44, Daniel 7:7,23-24, and Revelation 17:12-13). Since the time of the Roman Empire, there hasn't been a world-governing nation or empire. Napoleon, Hitler and Stalin tried, but they failed! There will be a short period coming when the world will be unified under one man. Daniel's dream featured a beast representing the Roman Empire with ten horns and a beast representing ten kings that will arise in the end time (Daniel 7:23-24). Revelation 13 describes the revival of a great military power.

4. An influential religious figure leads a religious revival. This spiritual leader will possess great charisma and will exercise a mighty influence over political power. He will unite all religions and is called the false prophet (Revelation 19:19-21).

5. The rise of a great false religious leader called the Antichrist (2 Thessalonians 2:3, 2 Thessalonians 2:8-9, Revelation 13:1).

6. The persecution of Jews and Christians will intensify (Revelation 12:17 and 14:12).

7. There will be an explosion of knowledge in the end times, and people will move about quickly (Daniel 12:4). Just think of how the world exponentially progressed in knowledge and technology over the past fifty years!

Conclusion

We are indeed sons and daughters of God, Almighty! God decided in advance to adopt us into His own family by bringing us to Himself through Jesus Christ. This is what He wanted to do, and it gave Him great pleasure. We praise God for the glorious grace He has poured out on us who belong to His Son *(read chapter 3 in my book CLOTHED FOR THE KING, which explains in detail how we belong to the King)*. God is so rich in kindness and grace that He purchased us with the blood of His Son and forgave our sins. He has showered His kindness on us, along with all wisdom and understanding (Ephesians 1:5-8). God wants us to be holy, which means to be separated or apart from the world and its wicked ways.

God's Word says we are either FOR or AGAINST Jesus Christ. Would you like to be invited to the marriage supper of Jesus, escaping all the turmoil and suffering on earth during the tribulation? If yes, it can happen for you right now! The first step is to say a prayer of repentance and accepting Jesus Christ as your Lord and Saviour. It is vital to understand that this prayer does not give you salvation! Jesus already forgave all your sins at the cross of calvary. The importance of this prayer lies in repentance and the acceptance of God's gift of salvation. Apostle Paul gave us the Gospel in 1 Corinthians 15:1-4, *"Moreover, brethren, I declare to you the Gospel which I preached to you, which also you received and in which you stand, by which also you are saved, if you hold fast that word which I preached to you-unless you believed in vain. For I delivered to you first of all that which I also received: that Christ died for our sins according to the Scriptures, and that He was buried, and that He rose again the third day according to the Scriptures."*

After saying this prayer, believe without a doubt that Jesus' sacrifice saved you. Then you have to commit to building your knowledge of God Almighty and getting to know Him. Pray the following prayer out loud and turn away from the sins of this world. Study the Bible regularly to get to know the true God and Creator of all!

Prayer of Salvation

Dear Jesus, I admit that I am a sinner.
I have done many things that don't please You.
I have lived my life for myself only.
I am sorry, and I repent. I ask You to forgive me.
I believe that you died on the cross, was buried and that
You rose again on the third day!
Please wash me in Your precious Blood and cleanse me
from all sin,
and write my name in the Lamb's Book of Life.
You did what I could not do for myself.
I come to You now and ask You to take control of my life.
From this day forward, help me to live every day for You,
and in a way that pleases You.
Please fill me with Your Holy Spirit!
Thank you, Father God,
for Your love and grace that brought me back to You.
Thank you, Jesus,
for Your great love in dying a humiliating,
and painful death for me!
Thank you, Holy Spirit,
for teaching and guiding me
back to the arms of my loving Father,
and King Brother in heaven.
I pray this in the beautiful name of Jesus Christ.
Amen and Amen!

Final Quote

'Making it to heaven and living in all eternity, should be our Ultimate Goal.'

I hope and pray to meet you, who have read this book, in heaven one day!

Love in Christ

Ellen Joubert

Dream Interpretation Symbols With Possible Meanings

A quick reminder here that each person or child has their dream language with God. All these possible meanings are just that, 'possible meanings'. I have asked God to make it easier for me since I've created these possible meanings for myself and to please give me dreams in line with what I can understand. It would be fantastic if we could understand Him all the time. On the other hand, God is Sovereign, and we cannot tell Him how we want things to be but can ask Him with a humble heart to speak to us in more straightforward terms, and most likely from our possible dream interpretation meanings.

Animals

Alligator – ancient, evil out of the past, danger, destruction, aggression, evil spirit that wants something you have or kill you.

Bat – evil spirit, witchcraft, evil spirit causing fear.

Bear – strength, judgment, evil spirit that wants something you have or kill you, economic loss (as in 'a bear market'), Russia.

Polar Bear – religious spirit.

Bird – a symbol of spirits (can represent good or evil). For example: a crow represents evil, and an eagle represents good. Many times an eagle represents God or the United States of America.

Bull - persecution, spiritual warfare, opposition, accusation, slander, threat, economic increase (as in a 'bull market').

Camel - endurance, long journey.

Cat - unclean spirit, stubborn, untrainable, predator, bewitching, charm, stealthy, sneaky, or deceptive, something precious in the context of a personal pet.

Black Cat - witchcraft, or evil.

Cheetah - danger, swift or fast, predator, play on the word for 'Cheater'.

Chicken - fear, cowardliness, a hen can mean protection, gossip, motherhood, a rooster can be boasting, bragging, proud, a chick can be defenceless, innocent.

Colt - bearing the burden of others or stubbornness.

Crab - not easy to approach.

Crow (raven) - confusion, unclean, operating in envy or strife, hateful, unclean, God's minister of justice, or provision.

Cow - subsistence, prosperity

Deer - graceful, swift, sure-footed, agile, timid.

Dog - unbelievers, religious hypocrites, loyalty, friendship, or faithfulness.

Pit Bulldog - ferocious demonic spirit.

Donkey - gentle strength, burden bearer, negative: stubborn.

Dove - Holy Spirit, peace.

Dragon - Satan.

Dinosaur - old stronghold, demonic, danger from the past, generational stronghold.

Eagle – prophetic, prophetic calling, USA, *Philippines (Philippine Eagle)*, Scotland and Mexico *(Golden Eagle)*, Namibia *(African Fish Eagle)*, etc.

Elephant – invincible or thick-skinned, not easily offended, powerful, extensive, having a significant impact, storing memory, old memory, long pregnancy.

Fish – souls of men, provision.

Fox – cunning, evil men, evil spirit, sly, sneaky, something that steals from you.

Frog – a spirit of lust, demon, curse, witchcraft.

Goat – sinner, unbelief, stubborn, argumentative, no discernment, negative person, being blamed for something (as in 'scapegoat').

Hawk – predator, sorcerer, evil spirit.

Horse – power, strength, conquest, spiritual warfare.

White Horse – salvation, rescue, redeem, royalty (Revelation 19:1).

Black Horse – feminine, bad times, evil (Revelation 6:5).

Red Horse – persecution, anger, danger, opposition (Revelation 6:4).

Leopard – swiftness, sometimes associated with vengeance, predator, danger.

Lion – Jesus (Lion of the tribe of Judah), royalty, kingship, bravery, confidence, Satan seeks to destroy.

Mice – something small that brings destruction, devourer, curse, plague, timid.

Mole – spiritual blindness.

Monkey – foolishness, clinging, mischief, dishonesty, addiction.

Mountain Lion – Satan, enemy, predator seeking to destroy.

Octopus – Jezebel Spirit because of the tentacles.

Ox – slow change, subsistence.

Black Panther – high-level witchcraft, demonic activity, works in darkness.

Pig – ignorance, hypocrisy, religious unbelievers, unclean people, selfish, vicious, vengeful.

Ram – sacrifice, God will provide.

Rat – unclean spirit, invader, destroyer *(feeds on garbage or impurities)*.

Raven – evil spirit, Satan.

Serpent – Satan, evil spirits.

Sheep – the people of God, innocent, vulnerable, humility, submission, sacrifice.

Skunk – stinking situation, unforgiveness, bitterness, bad attitude.

Snake – deception, lies, Satan, unforgiveness, bitterness.

White Snake – a spirit of religion, occult.

Sparrow – God will look after you, God will provide, small value but precious.

Tiger – danger, powerful ministry *(can be both good or evil)*, soul power, demonic spirit.

Tortoise – slow-moving, slow change, steady, old, old way of doing something, wise.

Turkey – foolish, clumsy, dumb, thanksgiving.

Vulture – scavenger, unclean, impure, an evil person, greedy, evil spirit.

Whale – significant impact in the things of the Spirit, going deep in the Spirit, disobedience, message from God.

Wolf - Satan or evil spirit, false ministries or false teachers, a predator.

* Animals in a dream can also represent emotions or certain characteristics.

Body Parts

Arm - strength, faith, rule.

Bald Head - lacking wisdom.

Beard - maturity.

Fingers - Thumb - apostolic, Pointer - prophetic, Middle - evangelistic, Ring - pastor, Pinky - teaching.

Hair - wisdom, anointing, glory (2 Corinthians 3:18).

Hand - relationship, healing.

Immobilized Body Parts - spiritual hindrance, demonic attack.

Nakedness - Positive: being transparent, humility, innocent. Negative: lust, temptation, in or of the flesh.

Neck - Positive: support or strength. Negative: obstinate, stubborn.

Nose - discernment.

Side - relationship, friendship.

Teeth - wisdom, comprehension, understanding.

Eye Teeth - revelatory understanding.

Wisdom Teeth - the ability to act in wisdom.

Thigh - faith.

Buildings & Places

Amphitheatre - magnification, being heard.

Atrium – light or growth from heaven.

Auto Repair Shop – ministry restoration, renewal, repair.

Back Porch – history, past.

Barn/warehouse – a place of provision and storage.

Castle – authority, fortress, a royal residence.

Church – where we learn, where we seek God, where God dwells, presence of God, presence of Jesus, presence of the Holy Spirit.

Country General Store – provision, basics, staples.

Elevator – changing position, going up in the spiritual realm, elevated, going down means demotion, trial, backsliding.

Farm – a place of provision.

Foundation – important foundational issues, established, stable or unstable *(depending on the context)*, the gospel, sound doctrine, church, government.

Front Porch – vision, future.

Garage – place to rest and refresh, place of protection, covering for ministries or people.

Garden – a person's heart, love, intimacy, growth.

Gas Station – receiving power, refilling or refuelling of the Spirit, empowering.

Hallway – transition that is usually direct or without deviation.

High-rise Building – high spiritual calling or high spiritual perspective.

Hospital – a place of healing, anointing.

House – person, family, ministry, church.

Previous/Old Home – past, inheritance, memory, revisiting old issues. Buying, or living in, the house of a known person in the ministry may mean that God has a similar call on your life.

Two-story House – double anointing.

Hotel – transition, a temporary place, a place to relax or receive blessings.

Jail/Prison – bondage, rebellion, addiction. Prisoners – may mean lost souls or persecuted saints.

Library – learning, building knowledge, research.

Mall – marketplace, provision for all your needs. Negative: self-centeredness, materialism.

Mobile Home/Trailer House – temporary place, condition or relationship, movement, easily movable, poverty.

Mountain – a place of encountering God, obstacle, difficulty, challenge, God's Kingdom, nation.

Office building – getting things accomplished, productivity.

Park – rest, peace, leisure, God's blessing, state of vagrancy.

River – water symbolizes life, renewal, regeneration, the flow of your life, water cleanses. A calm river symbolizes a calm life or situation. A stormy river symbolizes a turbulent phase of your life. Swimming in the water represents your spiritual life. Water represents the Holy Spirit.

Roof – spiritual covering.

School/Classroom – training period, a place of teaching, teaching ministry, teaching anointing.

Shack – poverty.

Stadium – a place of tremendous impact.

Staircase – Going up means promotion, Going down means: demotion, backsliding, failure, heavenly portal, up or down in the spirit and anointing, steps that need to be taken.

Swimming Pool – a place of spiritual refreshing, an area of God's Spirit, immersed in God, dirty water can indicate spiritual pollution, corruption, or backslidden condition.

Tent – a temporary place of rest, a meeting place with God.

Theater – on display, visible, going to be shown something, clarity, spiritual sight.

Windows – vision, letting light in, spiritual sight, opportunity *(open window of opportunity)*.

Zoo – strange, chaos, commotion, a busy place, noisy, strife.

Clothing

Bathrobe – coming out of a place of spiritual cleansing.

Cultural Clothing – missionary calling, prayer calling for a particular country or ethnic group.

Clothing not fitting – walking in something you're not called to.

Coat – mantle, superior, anointing.

Missing pants or another clothing piece – the feeling of lacking something.

Pyjamas – spiritual slumber.

Swimwear – ability to move in the Spirit.

Speedo – to move fast in the Spirit.

Shorts – a walk or calling that is partially fulfilled.

Shoes – Gospel of peace.

Tattered Clothing – mantle or anointing not being taken care of.

Wedding Dress - covenant, deep relationship with God.

Beautiful clothing piece that you are wearing in a dream - can mean we are wearing Jesus *(we are found in Christ - Romans 13:14)* and Galatians 3:27 say 'put on the Lord Jesus Christ.', 'clothe ourselves with Christ'.

Colours

Black - darkness, sin, earth, affliction, humiliation, calamity, death, mourning, mystery. Negative: sin, darkness.

Blue - heaven, authority, healing, flesh, revelation, communion, sky blue represents the Holy Spirit or the presence of Yahweh (God), represents the Word of God. Negative: depression, sorrow, anxiety.

Brown - compassion, humility. Negative: compromise, end of the season, rags, people, pride, weary, faint.

Cyan - mind, emotions, will.

Gold/Amber - glory, divinity, kingship, eternal deity, foundation, altar, beauty, precious, holiness, majesty, righteousness, purity. Negative: idolatry, blasphemy, licentiousness.

Green - growth, renewal, prosperity, consciousness, peace, symbolic of resurrection, represents the Holy Spirit. Negative: envy, jealousy, pride.

Grey - maturity, honour, wisdom. Negative: weakness.

Magenta - mind, emotions, will.

Orange - praise, harvest, perseverance, represents the Fire of God, deliverance. Negative: stubbornness.

Pink - this colour is a combination of red and white, childlike, love of God, Right relationship with God, anointing. Negative: childishness.

Purple/indigo - kingship, authority, royalty or priesthood, wealth, provision. Negative: false authority.

Rainbow Colours together – represents God, covenant.

Red – the blood of Jesus, love of God, atonement, salvation, righteousness, wisdom, anointing, power, love, flesh, mankind, represents the Holy Spirit. Negative: anger, war.

Sapphire – law, commandments, grace, the Holy Spirit, divine revelation.

Silver – purity, divinity, salvation, truth, atonement, grace, redemption, Word of God. Negative: legalism.

Turquoise – river of God, sanctification, healing, New Jerusalem.

White – righteousness, holiness, the bride of Christ, surrender, harvest, light, righteousness, conquest, victory, blessedness, joy, angels, saints, peace, completion, triumph. Negative: religious spirit.

Wine – new birth, multiply, overflow

Yellow – hope, mind, yellow is associated with fire, purification, faith, anointing, joy. Negative: fear, trials, cowards, pride.

Directions

East – Beginning (Genesis 11:2), Law (therefore blessed or cursed), birth, first (the sun rises in the east bringing a new day), false religions, the law of God (Psalm 103:12 'As far as the east *(law)* is from the west *(grace)*, so far hath He removed our transgressions from us').

East Wind – judgment, hardship (Genesis 41:23, 27; Exodus 10:13). *West* – End (a day end in the west with sunset), grace, death, last (Exodus 10:19). Luke 12:54 'And he said to the people when you see a cloud *(glory)* rise out of the west *(grace of God)*, straightaway ye say, There cometh a shower *(blessing)*, and so it is.'

North – God's judgment will come down (Jeremiah 1:13-14), Heaven or heavenly, spiritual warfare, dry time (Deuteronomy 2:3), Brings forth rain (Proverbs 25:23).

South - sin, world, temptation, trial, flesh, corruption, deception (Joshua 10:40; Job 37:9).

Right - In the natural: authority, power, man's strength *(flesh)* or the power of God revealed through man, accepted, place of favour (Matthew 5:29-30; Genesis 48:18; Exodus 15:6; Matthew 25:33; 1 Peter 3:22).

Right Turn - In the natural: change.

Left - Spiritual: Weakness *(of man)*, God's strength or ability demonstrated through man's weakness, rejected (Judges 3:20-21; Judges 20:16; Matthew 25:33).

Left Turn - Spiritual: change.

Back - past *(back door)*. Previous event or experience *(good or evil)*, that which is behind *(for example, past sins or the sins of our ancestors)*, unaware, unsuspecting, hidden, memory (Genesis 22:13; Joshua 8:4; Philippians 3:13).

Front - now or the future *(front yard or front porch)*, a prophecy of future events, immediate, current (Revelation 1:19 'Write the things which thou hast seen, and the things which *(presently)* are *(before, or in front of you)*, and the things which shall be hereafter.')

Food

Apples - spiritual fruit, temptation, something precious like the apple of God's eyes.

Bread - Jesus Christ *(who is the 'bread of life')*, Word of God, source of nourishment, God's provision.

Butter - extra, blessings, more than enough.

Chicken - a biblical bird found in Noah's ark, which symbolizes the Holy Spirit, love, God's forgiveness.

Fruits - Fruit of the Holy Spirit, Spiritual gifts.

Grapes – fruitfulness, success in life, evidence of being connected to Christ (John 15).

Honey – sweet, strength, wisdom, Spirit of God, the abiding anointing, the precious Word of God, the best of the land, abundance.

Lemons – sour, not too pleasant. Positive: building immunity.

Manna – God's miraculous provision, something is coming directly from God, the glory of God, the bread of life.

Meat – spiritually maturity, depth of God's Word.

Milk – good nourishment, elementary teaching of God's Word, new Child of God.

Pears – long life, pear trees have a long life, enduring much without complaining.

Pumpkin – Positive: change of the seasons, harvest time, a symbol of affection (as in 'you are my little pumpkin'), Negative: witchcraft, deception, snare, witch, trick (as in Halloween 'trick or treat').

Seed – represents the Word of God, a new beginning.

Strawberries – goodness, excellence in nature and virtue, healing, sweet, and very humble.

Tomato – kindness, the heart of God, big-hearted, generous.

Water – Holy Spirit, refreshing, Word of God, spiritual life.

Wine – Positive: working of the Spirit of God, move of God, Negative: drunkenness, love of the world, fleshly desires.

Eggs – the potential of new beginnings.

Ketchup – may mean to catch up with something or someone.

Bananas – Fruit of the Spirit, love, compassion.

Insects

Ant - industrious, wise, diligent, provision, hard work, teamwork, excellent communication, productivity, nuisance, stinging.

Bee/hornet - painful, evil spirit, strong demonic attack.

Butterfly - represents freedom, flighty, fragile, temporary glory, transformation.

Cockroach - infestation, unclean spirits, hidden sin.

Flies - evil spirits, the filth of Satan's kingdom, they live on dead things, occult.

Grasshopper - destruction, drought, pestilence.

Moth - a symbol of destruction, deception (as a moth drawn to the flame).

Scorpion - evil spirits, evil men, a pinch of pain.

Spider - occult attack, witchcraft.

Spider Web - a place of demonic attack, ensnaring, a trap, cursed.

Mantis - represent praying, you must spend more time praying.

Jewels and Valuables

Gold/Silver - they are products of God, not the creation of man. May mean precious, favour, going through a test, spiritual purity and glory, God is purifying and refining us (Zechariah 13:9). Dreaming of streets of gold refers to heaven (Revelation 21). In the Bible, silver is associated with knowledge, redemption, refining, idolatry, or even spiritual adultery.

Diamond - may mean commitment, purity, valuable, hardness, strong. Diamonds in dreams may also symbolize human beings. We are often said to be 'diamonds in the rough' in the Scripture, diamonds are referred to as precious stones (Exodus 28:18; Exodus 39:11; Ezekiel 28:13)

Emerald - the Bible lists it as one of the gemstones found in the High Priest's breastplate. Also, the fourth foundational stone in the New Jerusalem (Revelation 21:19). To dream of a coloured gemstone may even refer to the meaning of the colour. An emerald is green, and green can mean growth, prosperity, etc.

Pearls - according to the Bible, pearls play an integral role in the creation of the New Jerusalem for God's people. The twelve gates of the city are made of pearls (Revelation 21:21). It is the second most referenced gemstone in the entire KJV Bible. May also mean precious, favour, loyalty.

Rubies - are hard rock, precious, can also mean you have to refer to the red colour for the meaning in your dream.

Crown - indicated the presence of honour in the Old Testament. Jesus will one day reward His saints with crowns (1 Peter 5:1 - 4). The crown of holiness. Crowns are sometimes mentioned as a symbol of achievement or a sign of joy and gladness (Proverbs 4:9).

Rings – were symbols of authority and honour. Kings would often wear rings to symbolize their status and power. The father said to his servants, "Hurry! Bring out the best robe, and put it on him. Put a ring on his finger and sandals on his feet" (Luke 15:22). It may also mean commitment.

Chain around the neck - Daniel was honoured by placing a gold chain around his neck to honour and promote him.

Losing jewellery – may mean one is losing honour and favour.

Miscellaneous

Branches – represent God's People.

Christmas – spiritual gifts, the season of rejoicing, gifts from God, surprise, goodwill, benevolence, commercialism.

Choking – hindrance of some sort, difficulty accepting something *(the news was hard to swallow)*, hatred or anger, unfruitful *(for example, the weeds growing up and choking the plants)*.

Chewing - thinking on something *(I need to chew on that)*, meditating, receiving wisdom and understanding.

Difficulty Chewing - hard to say something, difficulty receiving something.

Dancing - usually God/Jesus dances with us in a dream to show us He wants to love us, have fun with us and do life together with us. His heart desires to have a relationship, conversation, intimacy, friendship, love with us.

Fire - Spiritual cleansing may mean you are playing with fire, representing Holy Spirit, determination and power, love, hate, passion for something, anger, fire can mean loss, fire can also mean godliness or connection to faith. A fire that hurts can be negative.

Flying - calling or the ability to move in the higher things of God, understanding the spirit realm of God.

Kiss - coming into agreement, covenant, seductive process, enticement, deception, betrayal, betrayal from a trusted friend.

Life seasons - may include former places you have been or lived, former schools, tests, jobs, etc. Reflecting on the significance of that season.

Pregnancy - is the process of reproducing, preparatory stage, the promise of God, Word of God as seed, prophetic word, desire, anticipation, expectancy, purposes of God preparing to come forth.

Purse or wallet - losing a purse or wallet can mean financial loss, or a person lost status, purpose, or identity.

Mirror - 2 Corinthians 3:18 says: 'As in a mirror the glory of God changes me'. A mirror is also where we are looking at ourselves.

Miscarriage - losing something at the preparatory stage, whether good or bad, plans aborted.

Repeating activities - God establishing a matter or issue, repeating something because you are not listening.

Running - faith, perseverance, working out one's salvation, moving forward with purpose.

Sea – representing people.

Swimming - living in the Spirit, moving in the things of the Spirit, operating in the gifts of the Spirit.

Taking a photo - transformation, transferring us into a new creation or dimension, God's picture of us is more magnificent than ours, God is transforming us more into His image, You are trying to capture or preserving something by taking a photo.

The Vine - represents Jesus.

Tree/s – representing God's people, a sign of God's provision, the Bible refers to itself as the 'Tree of Life' (Proverbs 3:18).

Wood - represents human nature *(it's considered a material that is corruptible and changeable as human nature)*. Jesus' profession on earth was a carpenter who was working with wood.

Numbers

1 - God

2 - Multiplication, division.

3 - Godhead *(Triune God)*.

4 - God's creative works, the universe (four winds/compass of the earth).

5 - Grace, redemption.

6 - Man.

7 - Perfection, completion.

8 - New beginnings *(Teacher)*.

9 - Judgment *(Evangelist)*.

10 - Journey, wilderness *(Pastor)*.

11 - Transition *(Prophet)*.

12 - The Church, God's redeemed people (*Apostle*).

13 - Rebellion.

14 - Double anointing.

15 - Reprieve, mercy.

16 - Established beginnings.

17 - Election.

25 - Begin ministry training.

30 - Begin ministry.

111 - My Beloved Son.

666 - Full lawlessness.

888 - Resurrection.

10,000 - Maturity.

Objects

Check - favour.

Credit Card - a presumption, lack of trust, attempting to walk in something you don't have yet, debt.

Crown - a symbol of authority, reign, a seal of power, Jesus Christ, honour, reward.

Fruited Trees - healing, the fruits of the Holy Spirit.

Gate - spiritual authority, entrance point for good or evil.

Key - spiritual authority, wisdom, understanding, ability, Jesus.

Ladder - ascending or descending, promotion or demotion, going higher into the things of God, a portal of heavenly activity *(as in Jacobs ladder had angels ascending and descending)*.

Microphone - influence, ministry, authority, being heard.

Microwave - impatience, quick work, convenient, sudden.

Mirror - God's Word, a person's heart, vanity.

Money - gain or loss of favour, power, provision, wealth, spiritual riches, authority, man's strength, covetousness, greed.

Phone call - is an ideal picture of connecting with the spirit world because we communicate without seeing them. A bad connection can mean there is interference from our side. God is always there on the other side!

Tree/s - symbolizes longevity, wisdom, and knowledge, leaders, mature believers.

Television - spiritual sight and understanding, entertainment, fleshly cravings and desires, fleshly spirit, love of the world.

People

Baby - new ministry or responsibility has recently been birthed, a new beginning, new idea, dependent, helpless, innocent, sin.

Bride - Christ's church, covenant, relationship.

Chef - The Holy Spirit preparing something for you.

Carpenter - Jesus, someone who makes or mends things, building something spiritually or naturally, preacher.

Family or People - in your dream, people you know may represent characteristics of them within you. Determine what the dominant personality of that person in your dream is.

Giant - Positive: godly men *(a giant of the faith)*, strong, conquer. Negative: demons, defilement *(like the Philistine Giant Goliath)*.

Harlot/Prostitute – a tempting situation, appealing to your flesh, worldly desire, a demon, spirit of lust, spiritual apostasy.

Hijacker – enemy wanting to take control of you or a situation, loss.

Husband – Jesus Christ, actual husband.

Lawyer – Positive: Jesus Christ, our advocate, mediator.

Negative: Satan, the accuser of the brethren, legalism.

Policeman – authority for good or evil, protector, spiritual authority, God is protecting us.

Prisoner – a lost soul, cursed.

Shepherd – Jesus Christ, pastor, leader *(good or bad)*, selfless person, protector.

Twins – Positive: double blessing or anointing. Negative: double trouble.

Rooms

Attic – mind, thought, history, past issues, family history, spiritual realm.

Basement – hidden, forgotten, hidden issues, foundation, basics.

Bathroom – spiritual cleansing, a prayer of repentance, confession of sins to another person.

Bathroom in full view – humbling season, others aware of cleansing, transparency.

Bedroom – intimacy, rest, privacy, peace, covenant *(as in marriage)*.

Dining Room – partaking of spiritual food, fellowship.

Kitchen – represent preparation time, heart *(the kitchen is known as the heart of the home)*, spiritual preparation, going deep in the Word of God, spiritual food, and feasting.

Restaurant or cafe – teaching ministry, more significant influence or impact, preparing to serve people, the Word of God.

Toilet – Feeling a need to go may mean you need to go in the natural, spiritually you may need to eliminate unnecessary waste in your life like unforgiveness, worries, etc.

Transportation

Most transport has to do with your ministry or calling.

Aeroplane – *(size and type of plane correlate to the interpretation)* prophetic ministry, going to heights in the Spirit, new and higher understanding.

Armoured Car – protection of God.

Automobile – personal ministry or job.

Bicycle – individual ministry or calling requiring perseverance.

Bus – church or ministry.

Car – your ministry or calling, ability to effectively make decisions in a given situation, a car takes you from one point to another.

Chariot – significant spiritual encounter.

Coal Car – on track, being directed by the Lord.

Convertible – open heaven in your ministry or calling.

Fire Truck – rescue, putting out fires of destruction.

Hang glider – going somewhere in the Spirit, driven by the wind of the Spirit.

Helicopter – mobile, flexible, able to get in the Spirit quickly, a higher calling.

Limousine – Positive: being taken to your destiny in style. Negative: materialism.

Mini Van - concerning the family.

Motorcycle - fast, powerful, or manoeuvrable calling.

Moving Van - transition, change.

Ocean Liner - impacting large numbers of people.

Road or path - give attention to the road in your dream. A dirt road may symbolize a difficult journey ahead. A paved road may represent a comfortable life or journey ahead. An old road from your past can signify the past.

Riverboat - slow-moving ministry or calling that impacts many people.

Rollercoaster - Positive: a wild ride that God is directing, exciting, but temporary. Negative: a path of destruction that first appears exciting, an emotionally trying time with ups and downs.

Sailboats - powered by the wind of the Spirit.

Spaceship - to the outer limits *(spiritually speaking)*.

Speedboat - fast, exciting, power in the Spirit.

Submarine or subway - undercover and active, but not seen by many, a behind the scene kind of ministry, hidden ministry.

Taxi Cab - a shepherd or hireling for someone *(driver)*, paying the price to get where you are going *(passenger)*.

Tow Truck - ministry of help, gathering the wounded.

Tractor - slow power, may speak about a need to plough or plant.

Train - a movement of God, denomination.

Truck - ability to transport or deliver.

Tugboat - providing assistance, ministry of help.

Weapons

Knife - brutal attack or gossip on you, protection *(if you are holding it to defend yourself)*.

Sword - Word of God, far-reaching, authority, overcoming evil.

Gun - spiritual authority *(can mean good or bad)*, protection, when you are shot, is most likely a demonic attack.

Dart - curses, demonic attack, accuracy.

Arrow - Positive: the blessing of children, focus, specific message *(as in shooting an arrow with your life)*. Negative: accusation or curses from the enemy.

Shield - faith, protection, God's truth, faith in God.

Weather

Earthquake - upheaval, change *(by the crisis)*, God's judgment, disaster, trauma, shaking, shock.

Fog - clouded issues or thoughts, uncertainty, confusion, temporary.

Hail - judgement, destruction, bombardment.

Rain - blessing, cleansing *(clear rain)*, trouble from the enemy *(dirty rain)*.

Snow - blessing, refreshing, righteousness, purity, grace (Isaiah 55:10-11).

Dirty Snow - impurity.

Snow Drift - a barrier, hindrance, or opposition.

Snow Blizzard - the inability to see, a storm that blinds you or obstructs your vision.

Storms - disturbance, change, spiritual warfare, judgement, sudden calamity or destruction, turbulent times, trial, opposition.

White Storm - God's power, revival, the outpouring of the Holy Spirit.

Tornadoes - destruction, danger, judgement, drastic change, the winds of change *(negative or positive depending on the colour of the tornadoes)*.

Wind - change *(the winds of change are blowing)*. Positive: Holy Spirit. Negative: adversity.

Fire - Cleaning something Spiritually. It may also mean you are playing with fire. Fire can represent the Holy Spirit in your life, cleaning you of something. It can signify determination, love, hate, anger, loss. Fire can also mean Godliness and connection to faith. Burnt by fire is negative.

CLOTHED FOR THE KING

was written to guide the people of God to be clothed and prepared for our Lord Jesus Christ's return.

ISBN: Paperback 978-0-6485691-0-7
EPUB 978-0-6485691-1-4
MOBI 978-0-6485691-5-2

Through Knowledge We Build Our Confidence. With Confidence we Overcome all the Devil's Lies!

As a born-again Christian, Ellen Joubert gave her life to our Lord Jesus Christ as a young woman. In 1999 the Holy Spirit gave her revelation that she would be writing books in the future. After eighteen years of preparation, the Lord has given her the assignment of 'building His people's confidence'. In 2017 God revealed that through writing books and speaking engagements, she will help build His people's confidence. Who are God's people? Everyone on this earth. Even those who haven't come to the realisation yet.

The enemy of this world, Satan, is attacking God's people and especially children's minds with lies such as that they are unworthy, unloved, ugly, and do not belong. This book goes into some great truths from God's Word on how wonderfully you were made and how you belong to a loving Father in Heaven who wants to guide your life. He wants you to have confidence in Him, spiritually, in your life journey, and in yourself. God not only wants you to be well spiritually, but on all levels of life, including your countenance, appearance, mentally, and health-wise. Through knowledge, we build confidence, and with confidence, we overcome all the devil's lies and obstacles in life. As an added bonus, you'll receive a 'Five-Week Study Guide' at the back of the book, which you can complete on your own, as a family, in a Bible Study Group, or through a Connect Group.

Read Ellen's testimony in this book on how God guided her to write books to show His people how to improve their appearance and countenance for Him. This Christian book shows the Biblical proof of why our countenance and appearance are important to the Lord. Her published books 'Style Yourself with Confidence' and 'How to Look and Feel Younger for Longer' teach more on the physical side to help God's people grow in confidence regarding their appearance and health. 'Clothed for the King' explains the spiritual side.

Bibliography

All Bible verses mentioned in this book are taken from **www.biblegateway.com,** and **www.biblehub.com** and are from different Bible translations, which have the same meaning as the original Bible but are explained in a more modern way to bring the message across.

Dictionary: The online Merriam-Webster, www.merriam-webster.com

Every Student, *'History of the Bible - Who wrote the Bible?'*, Web, www.everystudent.com, 16th November 2018.

Carlin Lawrence, *Jesus Christ's Glorious Return to This Earth'*, Web, www.agairupdate.com, 3rd November 2020.

Pinelli, Richard, *'God vs Satan: The Battle of the Ages'*, Web, **www.lifehopeandtruth.com,** 4th November 2020.

Bradley, Michael, *'What is Jezebel Spirit and How it Operates'*, Web, **www.bible-knowledge.com,** 9th November 2020.

Prince, Dereck, *'The Structure of Satan's Kingdom'*, Web, YouTube, 9th November 2020.

Hammond, Seth, *'4 Differences Between Christianity & Islam'*, Web, www.christcov.org, 10th November 2020.

Purdy, Alicia, *'Are Mormons Christians? 7 Major Differences in Critical Theology'*, Web, **www.crosswalk.com,** 10th November 2020.

Ibbitson, Donald, *'12 Warning Signs That a Person is Under the Influence of a Jezebel Spirit'*, Web, **www.aandbcounseling.com,** 24th November 2020.

Landry, Curt, 'Jezebel and a Religious Spirit: 40 Signs You Are Being Destroyed', Web, www.curtlandry.com, 24th November 2020.

King, Patricia, *The Religious Spirit*', YouTube, 24th November 2020.

Christian Truth Centre, *The Spirit of Antichrist*', Web, www.christiantruthcenter.com, 25th November 2020.

Ong, Czarina, *Why Billy Graham considers himself 'the greatest failure of all men': 'Too much with men and too little with God*', Web, www.christiantoday.com, 11th December 2020.

Jeremiah, David, *The Bible by Dr David Jeremiah*', YouTube, 3rd January 2021.

Pease, Glen, *The Jewels of Heaven*', Web, www.sermons.faithlife.com, 3rd January 2021.

Dr Hugh Ross, *Mythbusters: God and Science - Part 1*', YouTube, 4th January 2021.

Focus on the Family, *Evidence for the Bible*', Web, www.focus onthefamily.com, 4th January 2021.

Rogers, Adrian, *Is the Bible Really the Word of God?*', Web, www.christianity.com, 8th January 2021.

Culp, Doug, Faith, The Magazine of the Catholic Diocese of Lansing, *Are All Religions Simply Different Paths to the Same God?*', Web, www.faith mag.com, 8th January 2021.

Biblical Meanings of Color, Web, www.color-meanings.com/biblical-meaning-colors, 1st April 2021.

Snyder, Michael, *Pope Claims All Religions Worship Same God*', Web, www.iskconnews.org, 30th April 2021.

Jeremiah, David, *What Kind of Rewards Will Believers Receive in Heaven?*', Web, www.davidjeremiah.blog, 15th May 2021.

www.ingramcontent.com/pod-product-compliance
Lightning Source LLC
Chambersburg PA
CBHW050314010526
44107CB00055B/2237